Small
HOME PLANS

GARLINGHOUSE

P9-AFT-012

Library of Congress No: 89-81345

ISBN: 0-938708-31-7

Canadian orders should be submitted to:

The Garlinghouse Company
20 Cedar Street North
Kitchener, Ontario N2H 2W8
(519) 743-4169

TABLE OF CONTENTS

Well-planned Saltbox with a Balcony

No. 19704

The saltbox evolved during the Colonial times to provide more upstairs living space than was offered by conventional Cape Cod style homes. Yet we've gone even further than our forebears in updating that same profile to gain additional living space in the already compact structure. The kitchen is strategically located out of traffic patterns of other rooms. Yet it's convenient to either the front entry or the garage. Note the stairway to the basement is accessible from the garage, increasing the amount of usable space for the main level rooms. The living-dining area sports a ceiling that rises two stories to the open balcony off the upstairs bedrooms. The bedroom on the main level functions well as a study.

First floor — 744 sq. ft.
Second floor — 432 sq. ft.
Basement — 728 sq. ft.
Garage — 300 sq. ft.
Deck — 70 sq. ft.

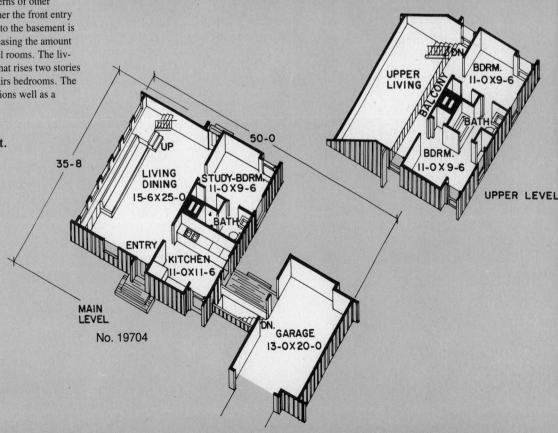

Master Retreat Crowns Spacious Home

No. 19422

Here's a compact beauty with a wide-open feeling. Step past the inviting front porch, and savor a breathtaking view of active areas: the columned entry with its open staircase and windows high overhead; the soaring living room, divided from the kitchen and dining room by the towering fireplace chimney; the screened porch beyond the triple living room windows. Tucked behind the stairs, you'll find a cozy parlor. And, across the hall, a bedroom with an adjoining full bath features access to the screened porch. Upstairs, the master suite is an elegant retreat you'll want to come home for, with its romantic dormer window seat, private balcony, and double-vanitied bath.

First floor — 1,290 sq. ft.
Second floor — 405 sq. ft.
Screened porch — 152 sq. ft.
Garage — 513 sq. ft.

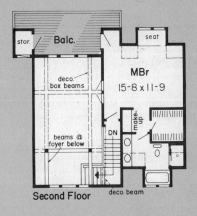

Second Floor

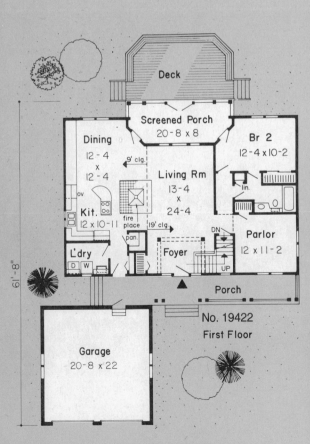

Deck

Screened Porch
20-8 x 8

Dining
12-4
x
12-4

9' clg.

ov

Kit.
12 x 10-11

L'dry
D   W

Living Rm
13-4
x
24-4

fire
place

19' clg.

pan.

DN

Foyer

UP

Porch

Br 2
12-4 x 10-2

lin.

Parlor
12 x 11-2

No. 19422
First Floor

Garage
20-8 x 22

61'-8"

3

Contemporary Ranch Design

No. 26740

Sloping cathedral ceilings are found throughout the entirety of this home. A kitchen holds the central spot in the floor plan. It is partially open to a great hall with firebox and deck access on one side, daylight room lit by ceiling glass and full length windows on another, and entryway hallway on a third. The daylight room leads out onto a unique double deck. Bedrooms lie to the outside of the plan. Two smaller bedrooms at the rear share a full bath. The more secluded master bedroom at the front has its own full bath and access to a private deck. A double garage completes the design. Crawl space construction is detailed.

Living area—1,512 sq. ft.
Garage—478 sq. ft.

Photos courtesy:
The American Wood Council
Washington, D.C.

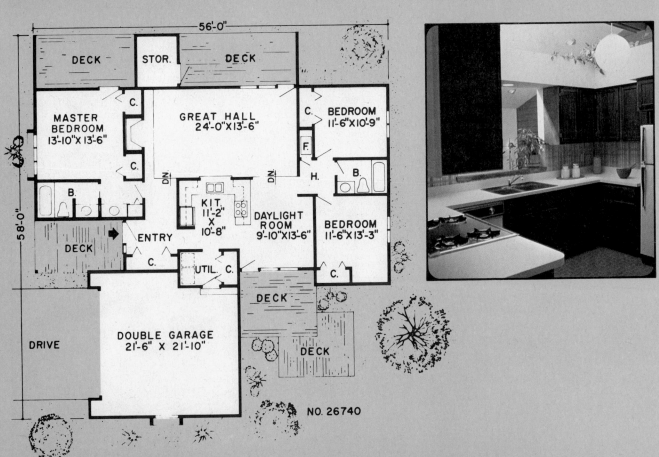

DECK   **STOR.**   **DECK**

56'-0"

58'-0"

MASTER BEDROOM
13'-10"X13'-6"

GREAT HALL
24'-0"X13'-6"

BEDROOM
11'-6"X10'-9"

C.

C.

C.

F.

B.

DN.

DN.

H.

B.

KIT.
11'-2"
X
10'-8"

DAYLIGHT ROOM
9'-10"X13'-6"

BEDROOM
11'-6"X13'-3"

DECK

ENTRY

C.

UTIL. C.

C.

DECK

DECK

DRIVE

DOUBLE GARAGE
21'-6" X 21'-10"

NO. 26740

Two-bedroom a Marvel of Livable Features

No. 19993

The extended entry deck is only a preface to the exciting and attractive features awaiting visitors to this home. Subtle divisions between the kitchen, dining and living areas create a sense of spaciousness, yet offer distinction of space. Cutouts on the upper level offer dramatic visualization from the master bedroom, study and second floor landing to the living room below. From the garage, entry into the kitchen provides convenience for unloading groceries and access to the dining / living room. For added convenience, the utility room is located just across the hall from the kitchen. Innovative design and lots of style make this small home a real beauty.

First floor—708 sq. ft.
Upper floor—525 sq. ft.
Garage & Storage—288 sq. ft.

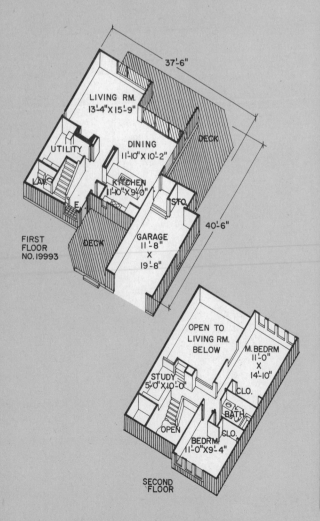

FIRST FLOOR NO.19993

LIVING RM.
13'-4" X 15'-9"

DINING
11'-10" X 10'-2"

DECK

UTILITY

LAV.

KITCHEN
11'-0" X 9'-0"

E.

STO.

DECK

GARAGE
11'-8"
X
19'-8"

37'-6"

40'-6"

SECOND FLOOR

OPEN TO LIVING RM. BELOW

M. BEDRM
11'-0"
X
14'-10"

STUDY
5'-0" X 10'-0"

CLO.

BATH

CLO.

OPEN

BEDRM.
11'-0" X 9'-4"

Hillside Haven

No. 19960

This wide-open charmer offers comfortable living for a
hillside location. Step up from the entry to an attractive
living and dining room combination warmed by a coal or
wood stove and lots of windows. The angular wall behind
the stove creates an interesting shape in the living room,
and in the handy kitchen on its other side. A short hall off
the entry leads to two bedrooms, each with a huge closet,
and a compartmentalized full bath. On the lower level,
you'll find a spacious solarium, a third bedroom, another
full bath, and a handy home workshop.

Upper level – 1,064 sq. ft.
Lower level – 1,064 sq. ft.
Garage – 420 sq. ft.

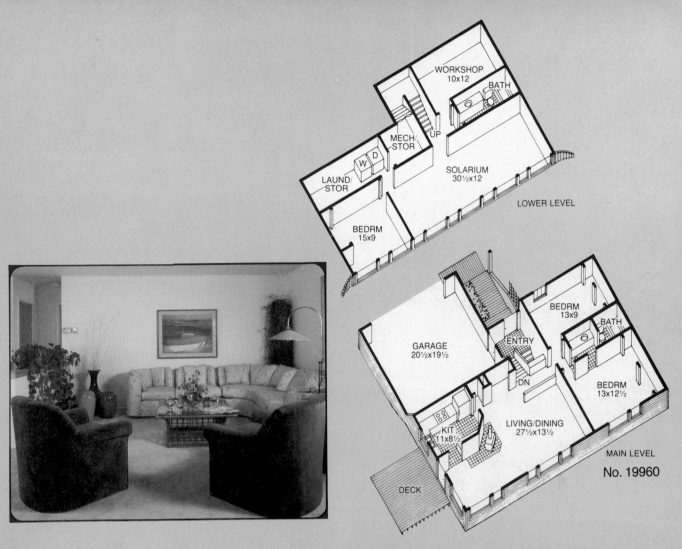

WORKSHOP
10x12

BATH

UP

MECH/
STOR

W D

LAUND/
STOR

SOLARIUM
30½x12

LOWER LEVEL

BEDRM
15x9

GARAGE
20½x19½

ENTRY

BEDRM
13x9

BATH

DN

BEDRM
13x12½

KIT
11x8½

LIVING/DINING
27½x13½

MAIN LEVEL

No. 19960

DECK

9

Arches Grace Classic Facade

No. 10677

Do you have a small lot, but love open space? Here's your answer! This compact beauty uses built-in planters and half-walls to define rooms without closing them in. Look at the first floor plan. The living room features a cozy sitting area dominated by a half-round window, then rises to nearly two stories for a wide-open feeling. At the rear of the house, the family room and kitchen, divided only by a cooktop peninsula, share the airy atmosphere. Sliders unite this sunny area with an outdoor patio that mirrors the shape of the dining bay. Peer down at the living room from your vantage point on the balcony that connects the three bedrooms upstairs. And, be sure to notice the double sinks and built-in vanity in the master bath, a plus when you're rushed in the morning.

First floor — 932 sq. ft.
Second floor — 764 sq. ft.
Garage — 430 sq. ft.
Basement — 920 sq. ft.

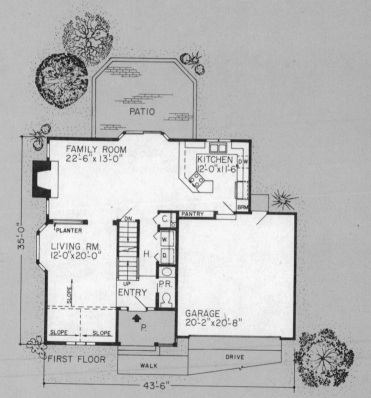

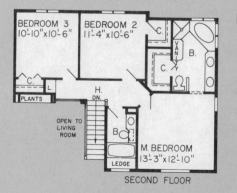

Wide-Open and Convenient

No. 20100

Stacked windows fill the wall in the front bedroom of this one-level home, creating an attractive facade, and a sunny atmosphere inside. Around the corner, two more bedrooms and two full baths complete the bedroom wing, set apart for bedtime quiet. Notice the elegant vaulted ceiling in the master bedroom, the master tub and shower illuminated by a skylight, and the double vanities in both baths. Active areas enjoy a spacious feeling. Look at the high, sloping ceilings in the fireplaced living room, the sliders that unite the breakfast room and kitchen with an adjoining deck, and the vaulted ceilings in the formal dining room off the foyer.

Main floor — 1,727 sq. ft.
Basement — 1,727 sq. ft.
Garage — 484 sq. ft.

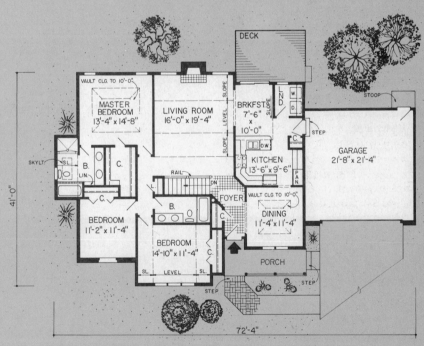

No. 20100   A Karl Kreeger Design

Stylish and Practical Plan

No. 20069

Make the most of daily life with a stylish and practical plan. The garage and seldom-used formal dining room separate the main areas of the house from traffic noise, while the rear of the home maximizes comfort and livability. The kitchen contains a breakfast area large enough for most informal meals and serves snacks to the living room or deck equally well. The spacious living room is a joy in either summer or winter thanks to the fireplace and broad views of deck and backyard. All bedrooms have plenty of closet space, and you'll especially appreciate the attic storage.

First floor — 1,313 sq. ft.
Second floor — 588 sq. ft.
Basement — 1,299 sq. ft.

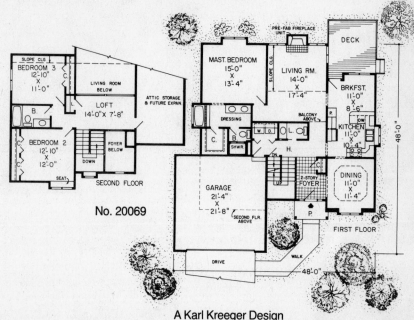

No. 20069

A Karl Kreeger Design

Trim Plan Designed For Handicapped

No. 10360

Attractive and accessible, this three bedroom home has been carefully detailed to provide both comfort and self-sufficiency for the handicapped individual. Ramps allow entry to garage, patio and porch. Doors and windows are located so that they can be opened with ease, and both baths feature wall-hung toilets at a special 16-18" height. Spacious rooms, wide halls, and the oversized double garage allow a wheel-chair to be maneuvered with minimal effort, and the sink and cooktop are also located with this in mind. Besides these functional aspects, the design also boasts a great room, inviting and open to the living areas and patio, supplied with a wood-burning fireplace. The sizable master bedroom merits an outside entry, both a convenience and safety measure, and adjoins a private bath with large shower accessible by wheelchair.

First floor — 1,882 sq. ft.
Garage — 728 sq. ft.

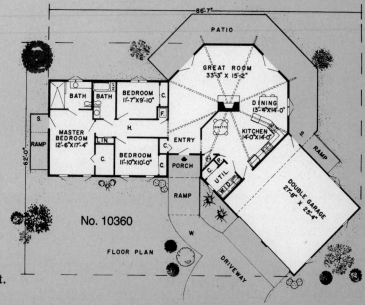

No. 10360

FLOOR PLAN

Elegant Entrance to Impressive Home

No. 20057

Two copper-roofed bay windows and a stone veneer front create an elegant entrance through an attractive circle head transom. Enjoy the vaulted ceilings that extend into the foyer, dining room, breakfast room, and master bedroom (with private dressing area). Even the kitchen is impressive with two separate eating areas and a connecting pantry for storage. Sliding glass doors from the breakfast room lead to a huge deck.

First floor — 1,804 sq. ft.
Basement — 1,804 sq. ft.
Garage & workshop — 499 sq. ft.

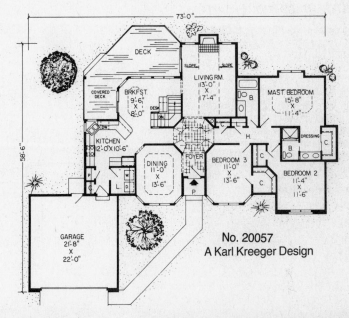

No. 20057
A Karl Kreeger Design

Bedroom Tower Creates Interesting Roof Line

No. 10618

Sloping ceilings and lofty open spaces are dominant features in this four-bedroom family home. Leading from the stairs to a full bath and two bedrooms, the upstairs hall is a bridge over the foyer and rustic living room. The dining room lies just off the foyer, adjacent to the island kitchen and breakfast room. The vaulted master suite with attached deck, a family bath, and bedroom with walk-in closet occupy a private wing.

First floor — 1,492 sq. ft.
Second floor — 475 sq. ft.
Garage — 413 sq. ft.

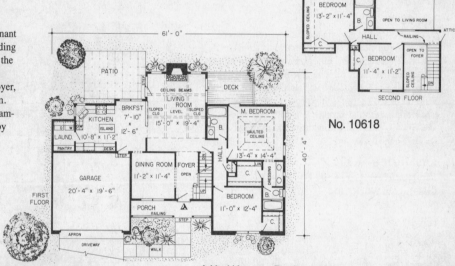

No. 10618

A Karl Kreeger Design

Living Room Focus of Spacious Home

No. 10328

Equipped with fireplace and sliding glass doors to the bordering deck, the two-story living room creates a sizeable and airy center for family activity. A well planned traffic pattern connects the dining area, kitchen, laundry niche and bath. Closets are plentiful, and a total of three 15-foot bedrooms are shown. A balcony overlooking the open living room is featured on the second floor.

First floor — 1,024 sq. ft.
Second floor — 576 sq. ft.
Basement — 1,024 sq. ft.

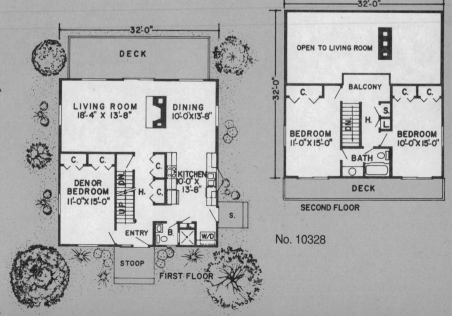

No. 10328

Classic Warmth

No. 10684

This compact traditional with clapboard exterior and inviting, sheltered entry boasts loads of features that make it a special home. Look at the built-in seat by the garage entry, the handy breakfast bar that separates the kitchen and family room, and the convenient powder room just off the foyer. Cathedral ceilings lend an airy quality to the living and dining rooms. A single step down keeps the two rooms separate without compromising the open feeling that's so enjoyable. Sliders lead from both dining and family rooms to the rear patio, making it an excellent location for an outdoor party. Tucked upstairs, the three bedrooms include your own, private master suite.

First floor — 940 sq. ft.
Second floor — 720 sq. ft.
Walkout basement — 554 sq. ft.
Garage — 418 sq. ft.
Crawl space — 312 sq. ft.

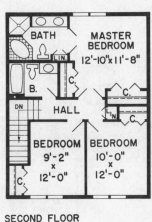

SECOND FLOOR

No. 10684

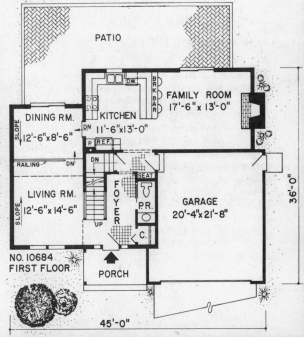

NO. 10684
FIRST FLOOR

Lots of Living in Four-bedroom Starter

No. 10520

This traditional exterior, with its charming dormers, provides four bedrooms and lots of style even on a small lot. The very large master suite on the second floor includes the luxury of a jacuzzi. The other second floor bedroom also has a private bath and a walk-in closet. On the first floor are two more bedrooms which share a bath. The living room is reminiscent of the old-fashioned parlor. The dining area and U-shaped kitchen are located toward the back of the house overlooking the lawn and provide an ideal setting for family meals.

First floor — 960 sq. ft.
Second floor — 660 sq. ft.
Basement — 960 sq. ft.

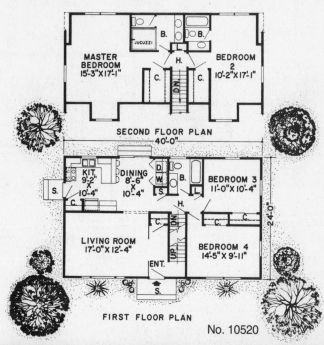

MASTER BEDROOM 15'-3" X 17'-1"

BEDROOM 2 10'-2" X 17'-1"

JUCUZZI

SECOND FLOOR PLAN 40'-0"

KIT. 9'-2" X 10'-4"

DINING 8'-6" X 10'-4"

BEDROOM 3 11'-0" X 10'-4"

LIVING ROOM 17'-0" X 12'-4"

BEDROOM 4 14'-5" X 9'-11"

ENT.

FIRST FLOOR PLAN

No. 10520

Simple Lines Enhanced by Elegant Window Treatment

No. 10503

Consider this plan if you work at home and would enjoy a homey, well lit office or den. The huge, arched window floods the front room with light. This house offers a lot of other practical details for the two-career family. Compact and efficient use of space means less to clean and organize. Yet the open plan keeps the home from feeling too small and cramped. Other features like plenty of closet space, step-saving laundry facilities, easily-cleaned kitchen, and window wall in the living room make this a delightful plan. It can be built on a slab foundation.

First floor — 1,486 sq. ft.
Garage — 462 sq. ft.
Basement — 1,486 sq. ft.

DECK

DINING 10'-8" X 11'-4"

LIVING ROOM 14'-8" X 21'-0" SLOPED CLG.

MAST. BEDROOM 13'-4" X 13'-8"

KITCHEN 10'-8" X 10'-0"

BEDROOM 13'-10" X 11'-4"

FOYER

DEN/BDRM 10'-4" X 11'-10"

GARAGE 20'-4" X 21'-4"

DRIVE

56'-0"

48'-0"

No. 10503

Impact Two-story Design
Ideal for Small Lot

No. 10517

On the second floor of this well-arranged home are two bedrooms which flank a bath that is illuminated by a skylight. Adjacent to the bath are individual dressing areas each with its own basin and large walk-in closet. The interesting angles incorporated into the plan of the first floor create extra space in the master suite. The living room has a sloped ceiling and a fireplace with tile hearth. The angular kitchen includes a pantry, space for a dinette set and direct access to the rear deck. Other features include a half bath on the first floor, a conveniently located laundry, and an inviting two-story foyer.

First floor — 1,171 sq. ft.
Second floor — 561 sq. ft.
Basement — 1,171 sq. ft.
Garage — 484 sq. ft.

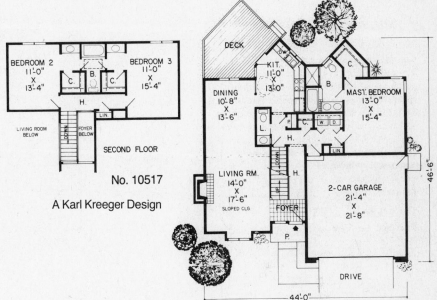

No. 10517

A Karl Kreeger Design

Intelligent Use of Space

No. 10483

Lots of living is packed into this well-designed home which features a combined kitchen and dining room. The highly functional U-shaped kitchen includes a corner sink under double windows. Opening onto the dining room is the living room which is illuminated by both a front picture window and a skylight. Its lovely fireplace makes this an inviting place to gather. The sleeping area of this home contains three bedrooms and two full baths, one of which is a private bath accessed only from the master bedroom.

First floor — 1,025 sq. ft.
Garage — 403 sq. ft.

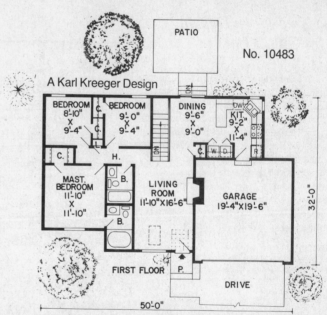

No. 10483

A Karl Kreeger Design

PATIO

BEDROOM 8'-10" X 9'-4"

BEDROOM 9'-0" X 9'-4"

DINING 9'-6" X 9'-0"

KIT. 9'-2" X 11'-4"

C.

MAST. BEDROOM 11'-10" X 11'-10"

B.

LIVING ROOM 11'-10"X16'-6"

GARAGE 19'-4"X19'-6"

B.

FIRST FLOOR

DRIVE

32'-0"

50'-0"

Compact Plans Offers Lots of Living Space

No. 10502

This three bedroom home, with its interesting exterior roof lines, opens to a well-designed family floor plan. Two bedrooms are separated on the second level while the master suite is secluded on the first floor. The master suite includes a five-piece bath with double vanity plus a full-wall closet. The remainder of the first floor encompasses a spacious living room complete with sloped ceiling, a hearthed fireplace and double windows. The dining room enlarges the living room and adjoins the U-shaped kitchen which is separated from the sunny breakfast room by a bar. The deck area provides a lovely area for outdoor family gatherings.

First floor — 1,172 sq. ft.
Second floor — 482 sq. ft.
Garage — 483 sq. ft.

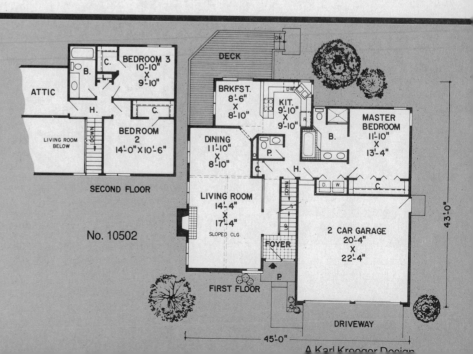

B.

ATTIC

BEDROOM 3 10'-10" X 9'-10"

DECK

LIVING ROOM BELOW

BEDROOM 2 14'-0"X10'-6"

SECOND FLOOR

No. 10502

BRKFST. 8'-6" X 8'-10"

KIT. 9'-10" X 9'-10"

DINING 11'-10" X 8'-10"

MASTER BEDROOM 11'-10" X 13'-4"

B.

LIVING ROOM 14'-4" X 17'-4"
SLOPED CLG

FOYER

2 CAR GARAGE 20'-4" X 22'-4"

FIRST FLOOR

DRIVEWAY

43'-0"

45'-0"

A Karl Kreeger Design

Fireplace in Living and Family Rooms

No. 9263

This beautiful ranch design features an extra large living room with plenty of formal dining space at the opposite end. Large wood-burning fireplaces are found in both the living and family rooms. A mudroom, located off the kitchen, features a laundry area, half bath, and storage closet. The charming master bedroom has a full bath and plenty of closet space.

First floor — 1,878 sq. ft.
Garage — 538 sq. ft.

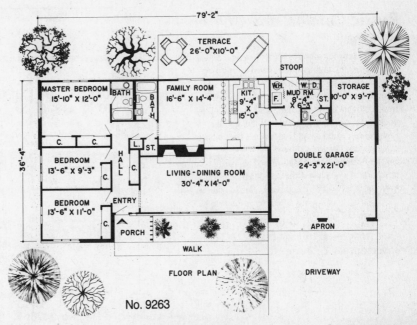

No. 9263

FLOOR PLAN

Rustic Comfort and Charm

No. 9076

Vacation in rustic comfort. Natural wood siding and a stone chimney highlight the charm of this plan. Sit back on the roomy front porch and enjoy old fashioned peace and quiet. And inside, where the fireplace lights the living and dining rooms, enjoy modern conveniences like the efficient kitchen, roomy closets, and enough bathrooms for a houseful of guests. The main floor of the house is designed compactly so that a retired couple faces a minimum of upkeep, yet the additional bedrooms offer plenty of room for company. Notice that the bedrooms close off tightly to conserve heating bills. This home can be built on a slab foundation.

First floor — 1,140 sq. ft.
Basement — 1,140 sq. ft.

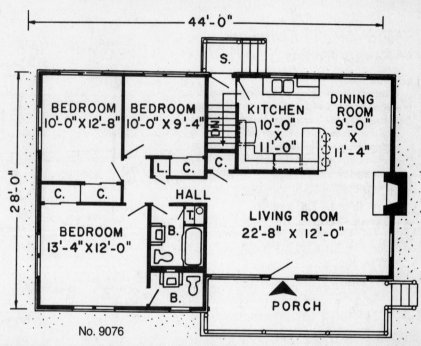

No. 9076

Green House Adds Charm and Warmth to Multi-Level Plan

No. 10468

The well-placed solar greenhouse is located on the lower level of this inviting design. Sliding glass doors open into the greenhouse from the family room while casement windows over the kitchen sink open into the space above. The master bedroom also has access to the outdoors through the sliding glass doors onto an elevated deck. Two additional bedrooms are located across the hall. The living room is warmed by a hearthed fireplace and adjoins the combined kitchen and dining areas.

Upper level — 1,294 sq. ft.
Family room level — 292 sq. ft.
Garage — 608 sq. ft.
Greenhouse — 164 sq. ft.

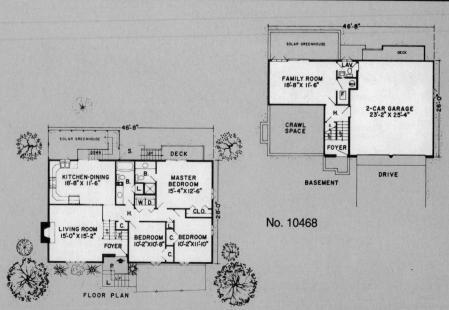

No. 10468

Perfect For Entertaining

No. 20050

As guests enter the two-story, tiled foyer, they are immediately welcomed by the expansive living room with its sloped ceiling and cheery fireplace. Lead them into the dining room and serve them from the adjacent kitchen. There's even room for more than one cook in this roomy kitchen which opens onto a covered deck for outdoor meals. The first-floor master bedroom features a large, five-piece bath and double closets. Upstairs are two more bedrooms with roomy closets, an additional bath and room for storage in the attic.

First floor — 1,303 sq. ft.
Second floor — 596 sq. ft.
Basement — 1,303 sq. ft.
Garage — 460 sq. ft.

No. 20050

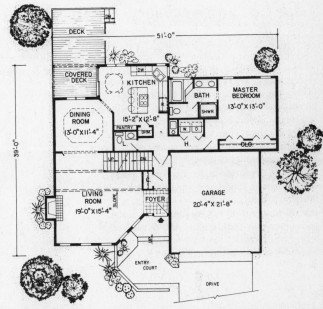

Cape Cod Passive Solar Design

No. 10386

A solar greenhouse on the south employs energy storage rods and water to capture the sun's warmth, thereby providing a sanctuary for plants and supplying a good percentage of the house's heat. Other southern windows are large and triple glazed for energy efficiency. From one of the bedrooms, located on the second floor, you can look out through louvered shutters to the living room below, accented by a heat circulating fireplace and a cathedral ceiling with three dormer windows which flood the room with light. On the lower level, sliding glass doors lead from the sitting area of the master bedroom suite to a private patio. Also on this level are a dining room, kitchen, mudroom, double garage with a large storage area and another larger patio.

First floor — 1,164 sq. ft.
Second floor — 574 sq. ft.
Basement — 1,164 sq. ft.
Greenhouse — 238 sq. ft.
Garage & storage — 566 sq. ft.

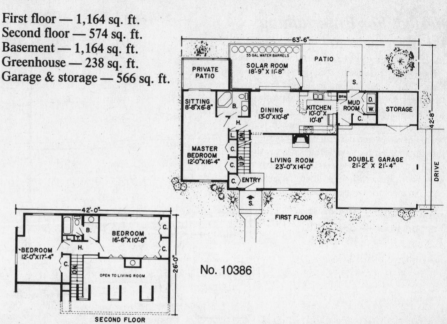

No. 10386

Fireplace a Feature

No. 9838

Family convenience is emphasized in this beautiful ranch style home. The owner's suite includes double closets and a private bath with a spacious built-in vanity. A two-way wood-burning fireplace between the living room and dining room permits the fire to be enjoyed from both rooms. An extra large garage possesses an abundance of extra storage space.

First floor — 1,770 sq. ft.
Basement — 1,770 sq. ft.
Garage — 700 sq. ft.

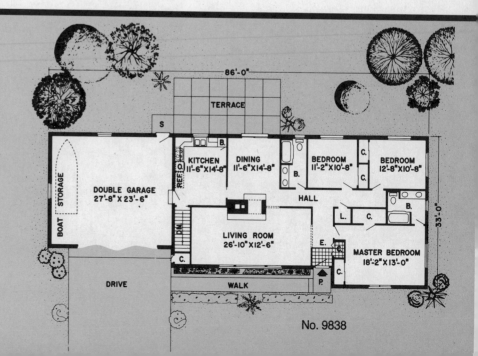

No. 9838

22

Angular Design is Strikingly Contemporary

No. 10469

The living room is the focal point of this contemporary design and incorporates several innovative features. Its vaulted ceiling is highlighted with exposed beams, and the angled front has up to four levels of windows which are operated by remote control. A wood-burning fireplace and built-in bookshelves enhance the rear wall of the room. The kitchen, informal serving area and dining room occupy the remainder of the first floor. The second floor is reserved for the three spacious bedrooms. The master bedroom also has a beamed ceiling plus its own fireplace.

First floor — 989 sq. ft.
Second floor — 810 sq. ft.
Garage — 538 sq. ft.

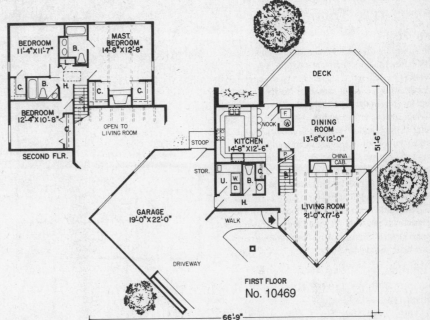

SECOND FLR.

BEDROOM 11'-4"x11'-7"

MAST. BEDROOM 14'-8"x12'-8"

BEDROOM 12'-4"x10'-8"

OPEN TO LIVING ROOM

DECK

GARAGE 19'-0" x 22'-0"

STOOP

STOR.

KITCHEN 14'-8"x12'-6"

NOOK

DINING ROOM 13'-8"x12'-0"

CHINA CAB.

LIVING ROOM 21'-0"x17'-6"

WALK

DRIVEWAY

FIRST FLOOR
No. 10469

51'-6"

66'-9"

Covered Porch Offered in Farm-type Traditional

No. 20064

This pleasant traditional design has a farmhouse flavor exterior that incorporates a covered porch and features a circle wood louver on its garage, giving this design a feeling of sturdiness. Inside on the first level from the foyer and to the right is a formal dining room complete with a bay window, an elevated ceiling, and a corner china cabinet. To the left of the foyer is the living room with a wood-burning fireplace. The kitchen is connected to the breakfast room and there is a room for the laundry facilities. A half bath is also featured on the first floor. The second floor has three bedrooms. The master bedroom, on the second floor, has its own private bath and walk-in closet. The other two bedrooms share a full bath. A two-car garage is also added into this design.

First floor — 892 sq. ft.
Second floor — 836 sq. ft.
Basement — 892 sq. ft.
Garage — 491 sq. ft.

A Karl Kreeger Design

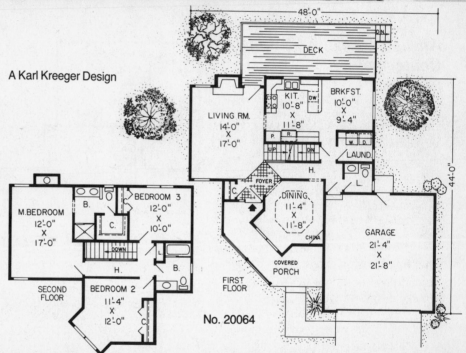

No. 20064

Carefree Convenience

No. 20402

Although this adaptable, one-level gem features handicapped accessibility, it's an excellent choice for anyone looking for an easy-care home. Notice the extra-wide hallways, the master bath with roll-in shower, and specially designed kitchen with roll-out pantry and counters designed for wheelchair access. A sunny, spacious atmosphere envelopes each room, thanks to generous windows and sloping ceilings. Reach the deck from the U-shaped kitchen overlooking the fireplaced family room, and from the master suite. The dining room and living room, separated by a handy bar and just steps away from the kitchen, are ideal for entertaining. A hall bath serves the front bedrooms.

Main living area — 2,153 sq. ft.
Garage — 617 sq. ft.

Floor Plan

No. 20402

Attractive Floor Plan Enhances Traditional Design

No. 20056

This three-bedroom, two-bath home offers comfort and style. The master bedroom is complete with its own bath with a skylight. A beamed ceiling and fireplace in the living area add charm to the more traditional family room. A spacious laundry room adjoins the kitchen and breakfast area. The country-style front porch and large front windows in the breakfast and dining rooms lend a cozy atmosphere to this eye-catching design.

First floor — 1,669 sq. ft.
Basement — 1,669 sq. ft.
Garage — 482 sq. ft.

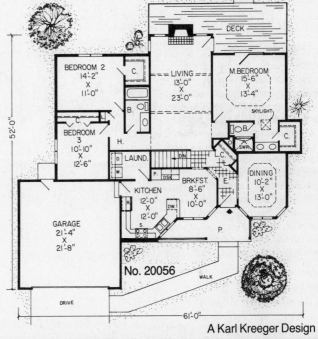

A Karl Kreeger Design

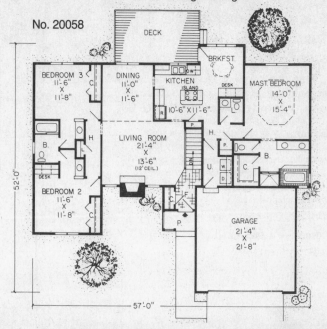

Ranch Incorporates Victorian Features

No. 20058

This wonderful Victorian-featured ranch design incorporates many luxury conveniences usually offered in larger designs. The master bedroom is expansive in size, with an oversized full bath complete with a walk-in closet, an individual shower, a full tub, and a two-sink wash basin. A large kitchen area is offered with a built-in island for convenience. The kitchen also has its own breakfast area. Located next to the kitchen is a half bath. The living area is separated from the dining room by a half-partition wall. Two large bedrooms complete the interior of the house. They have large closets and share a full bath. A two-car garage and a wood deck complete the options listed in this design.

First floor — 1,787 sq. ft.
Basement — 1,787 sq. ft.
Garage — 484 sq. ft.

No. 20058

DECK

BRKFST.

BEDROOM 3
11'-6" X 11'-8"

DINING
11'-0" X 11'-6"

KITCHEN
ISLAND
10'-6" X 11'-6"

DESK

MAST. BEDROOM
14'-0" X 15'-4"

B.

DESK

LIVING ROOM
21'-4" X 13'-6"
(12' CEIL)

B.

BEDROOM 2
11'-6" X 11'-8"

GARAGE
21'-4" X 21'-8"

52'-0"

57'-0"

Three Bedroom Features Cathedral Ceilings

No. 20051

The tiled foyer of this charming house rises to the second floor balcony and is lighted by a circular window. To the right of the foyer are the powder room, the compact laundry area, and the entrance to the well-designed kitchen. The kitchen features a central island, built-in desk, pantry, and adjacent breakfast area. The combined living and dining room enjoys a fireplace, built-in bookcase, and sloped ceiling.

First floor — 1,285 sq. ft.
Second floor — 490 sq. ft.
Basement — 1,285 sq.f t.
Garage — 495 sq. ft.

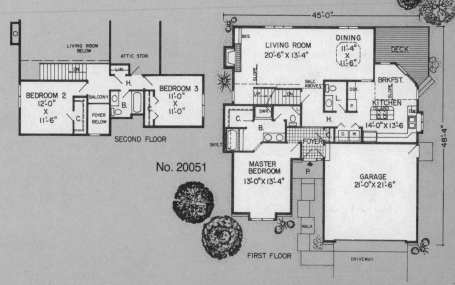

LIVING ROOM BELOW

ATTIC STOR.

BEDROOM 2
12'-0" X 11'-6"

BALCONY

FOYER BELOW

BEDROOM 3
11'-0" X 11'-0"

B.

SECOND FLOOR

45'-0"

LIVING ROOM
20'-6" X 13'-4"

DINING
11'-4" X 11'-6"

DECK

BRKFST.

BALC. ABOVE

KITCHEN
14'-0" X 13'-6"

FOYER

No. 20051

48'-4"

MASTER BEDROOM
13'-0" X 13'-4"

GARAGE
21'-0" X 21'-6"

WALK

FIRST FLOOR

DRIVEWAY

A Karl Kreeger Design

Options Abound

No. 20061

This striking exterior features vertical siding, shake shingles, and rock, to set off a large picture window. Inside, the kitchen has a built-in pantry, refrigerator, dishwasher and range, breakfast bar, an open-beamed ceiling with a skylight, plus a breakfast area with lots of windows. A formal dining room complements the living room, which has two open beams running down a sloping ceiling and a wood-burning fireplace. There is a laundry closet, and the foyer area also has a closet. Three bedrooms share a full bath. The master bedroom has an open-beamed, sloping ceiling with a spacious bath area and a walk-in closet.

First floor — 1,667 sq. ft.
Basement — 1,656 sq. ft.
Garage — 472 sq. ft.

A Karl Kreeger Design

Dramatic Shape and Features

No. 10274

If your lot is the right shape, build this magnificent plan. A dramatically positioned fireplace forms the focus of a contemporary living area. Kitchen, dining, and living spaces are fashioned into a huge central room that flows from the heart of the home through sliding doors to the dramatic deck. The many flexible decorating options, such as screens and room dividers or conversational groupings, are impressive. A huge master bedroom and two roomy bedrooms are tucked in a wing away from the main area for privacy.

First floor — 1,783 sq. ft.
Garage — 576 sq. ft.

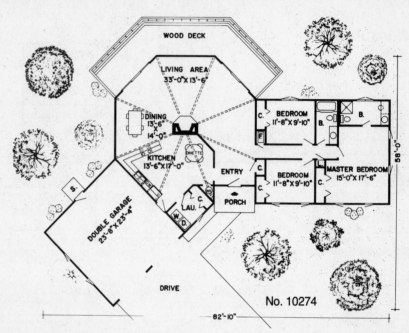

Screened Porch Designed For Dining

No. 8262

This three bedroom, two bath design has a screened porch adjacent to the dining room which offers sheltered open air-dining. A corner fireplace in the living room and the unique expanse of windows create a certain ambiance repeated in the airy, yet efficient kitchen. The master bedroom merits a full bath.

First floor — 1,406 sq. ft.
Basement — 1,394 sq. ft.
Garage — 444 sq. ft.
Screen porch — 107 sq. ft.

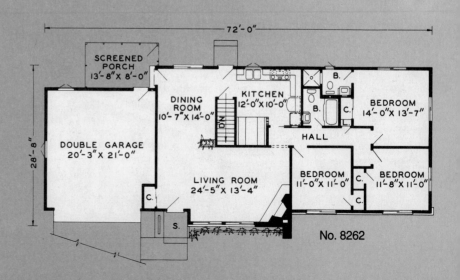

Sloped Ceiling is Attractive Feature

No. 10548

The fireplace and sloped ceiling in the family room offer something a bit out of the ordinary in a small home. The master bedroom is complete with full bath and a dressing area. Bedrooms two and three share a full bath across the hall, and a half bath is conveniently located adjacent to the kitchen. A walk-out bay window is shown in the spacious breakfast room, and a bay window with window seat has been designed in the master bedroom. The screened porch off of the breakfast room is an inviting feature for meals outside.

First floor — 1,688 sq. ft.
Basement — 1,688 sq. ft.
Screened porch — 120 sq. ft.
Garage — 489 sq. ft.

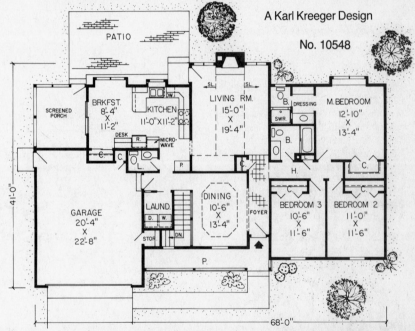

A Karl Kreeger Design

No. 10548

Rustic Exterior; Complete Home

No. 10140

Although rustic in appearance, the interior of this cabin is quiet, modern and comfortable. Small in overall size, it still contains three bedrooms and two baths in addition to a large, two-story living room with exposed beams. As a hunting-fishing lodge or mountain retreat, this compares well.

First floor — 1,008 sq. ft.
Second floor — 281 sq. ft.
Basement — 1,008 sq. ft.

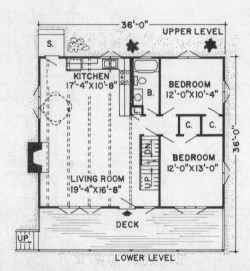

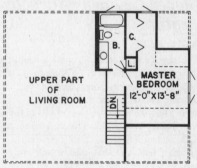

No. 10140

Master Suite Crowns Plan

No. 10394

The master bedroom suite occupies the entire second level of this passive solar design. The living room rises two stories in the front, as does the foyer, and can be opened to the master suite to aid in air circulation. Skylights in the sloping ceilings of the kitchen and master bath give abundant light to these areas. Angled walls, both inside and out, lend a unique appeal. An air-lock entry, 2x6 exterior studs, 6-inch concrete floor, and generous use of insulation help make this an energy efficient design.

First floor — 1,306 sq. ft.
Second floor — 472 sq. ft.
Garage — 576 sq. ft.

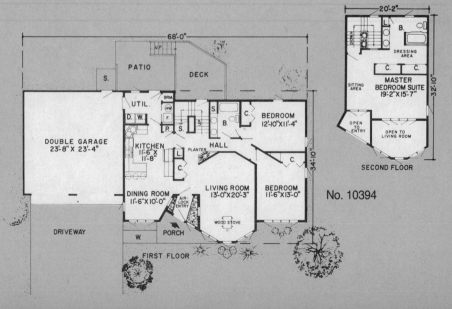

No. 10394

Simple Yet Elegant Lines
Enclose Livable Plan

No. 10484

This two-story home offers integrated living spaces for an active family. The front breakfast room is just across the counter from the efficiently organized kitchen which is highlighted by a bumped out window over the double sink. Neatly tucked between the kitchen and breakfast room is the laundry center. Adjacent to the kitchen is the dining room which flows into the living room and the warmth of its hearthed fireplace. Upstairs are three bedrooms including a generous master suite.

First floor — 869 sq. ft.
Second floor — 840 sq. ft.
Basement — 869 sq. ft.
Garage — 440 sq. ft.

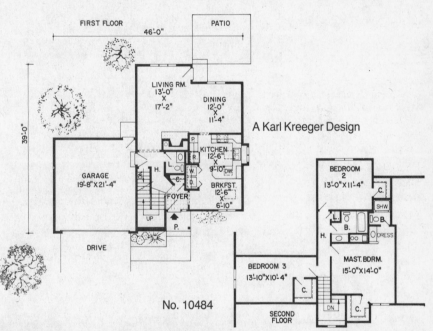

A Karl Kreeger Design

No. 10484

A Karl Kreeger Design

Outdoor-Lover's Dream

No. 20055

Here's a handsome home that presents a pretty face to passers-by, and provides lots of outdoor living space on a spacious rear deck. Soaring ceilings, oversized windows, and sliding glass doors unite the living room with the deck and rear yard. And, the handy kitchen makes meal service a breeze to the dining room, adjoining breakfast bay, or deck. Tucked upstairs for quiet and privacy, three bedrooms open to a skylit hallway. The dramatic master suite features soaring ceilings and a private dressing area flanked by a full bath and walk-in closet.

First floor — 928 sq. ft.
Second floor — 773 sq. ft.
Basement — 910 sq. ft.
Garage — 484 sq. ft.

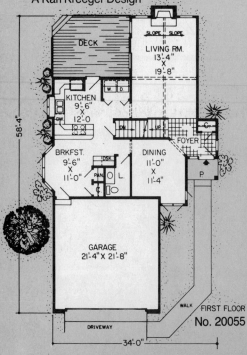

Tudor Sun Catcher

No. 90249

Face the rear of this efficient ranch home south to take advantage of the sun's free energy. The breakfast room, and the soaring living and dining rooms feature rear-facing glass walls, providing a sunny atmosphere enhanced by the warmth of a massive fireplace. The attached covered porch, accessible to both living and breakfast rooms, adds to the outdoor ambiance. The centrally located kitchen features a handy snack bar and built-in pantry and planning desk, just steps away from the storage area off the attached garage. You'll love the cheerful atmosphere in the three front-facing bedrooms, which share a private corner of the house with two full baths.

Main living area — 1,584 sq. ft.
Garage — 2-car

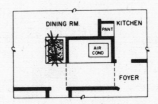

OPTIONAL NON-BASEMENT

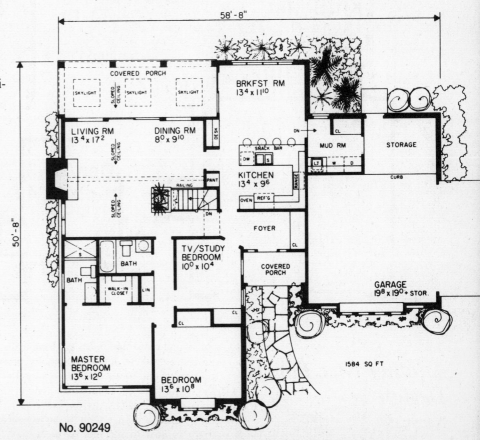

No. 90249

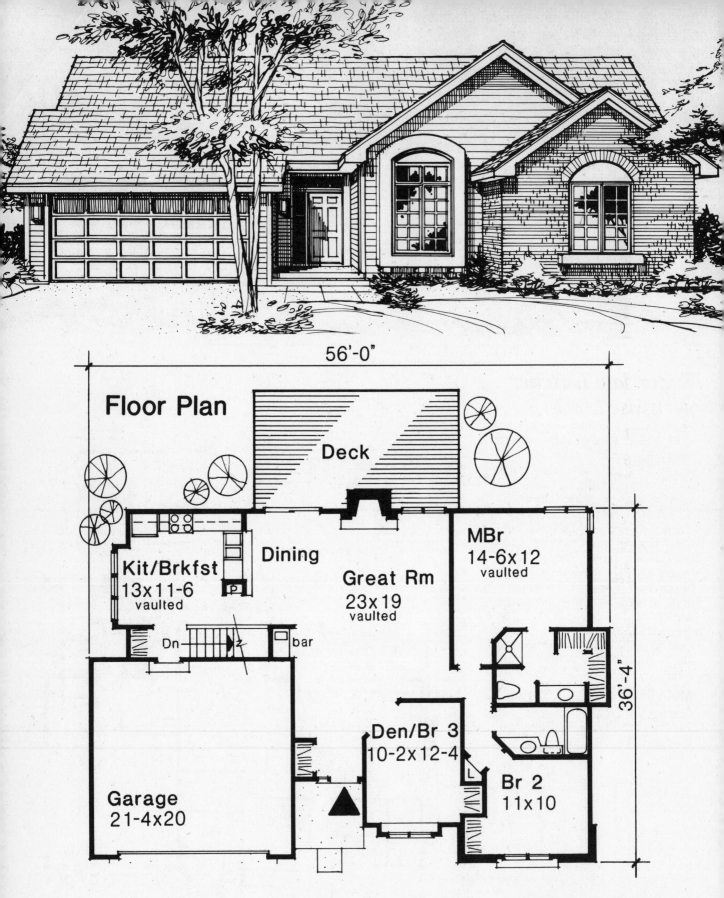

Floor Plan

56'-0"

Deck

Kit/Brkfst
13x11-6
vaulted

Dining

Great Rm
23x19
vaulted

MBr
14-6x12
vaulted

Dn   bar

36'-4"

Garage
21-4x20

Den/Br 3
10-2x12-4

Br 2
11x10

Another Nice Ranch Design

No. 90354

Small and move-up houses are looking much larger these days through their proportioning and roof massing as exemplified in this two-bedroom ranch. The inside space seems larger from the high-impact entrance with through-views to the vaulted great room, fireplace and the rear deck. The den (optional third bedroom) features double doors and the kitchen/breakfast area has a vaulted ceiling. the plan easily adapts to crawl or slab construction with utilities replacing stairs; laundry facing kitchen and air handler and water heater facing garage.

First floor — 1,360 sq. ft.

Victorian Touches Disguise Modern Design

No. 90616

Indulge in the romance of Victorian styling without sacrificing up-to-date living. Out of the past come porches with turned wood posts, exterior walls of round shingles, wonderful bay windows, and decorative scroll work. But the present is evident in the kitchen and family room, with a skylit entertainment area for today's electronic pleasures. The stairs begins its rise with a turned post and rail. The master suite features a high ceiling with an arched window, private bath, and tower sitting room with adjoining roof deck.

Basic house — 1,956 sq. ft.
Laundry — 36 sq. ft.
Garage — 440 sq. ft.
Basement — 967 sq. ft.

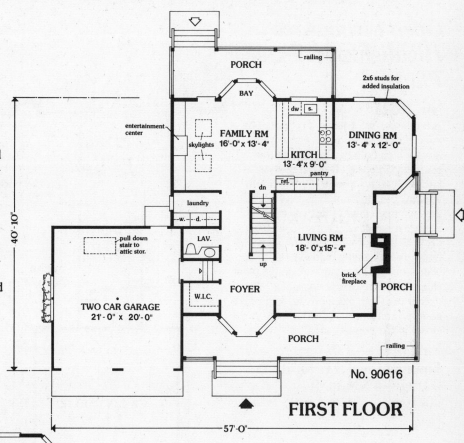

FIRST FLOOR

No. 90616

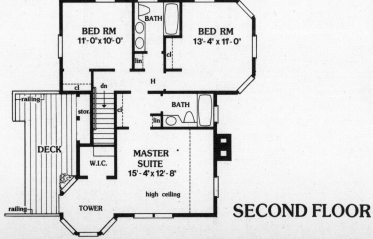

SECOND FLOOR

Open Living Area Highlights Well-zoned Plan

No. 10523

A feeling of spaciousness is created by the centrally located living and dining areas which both have a view of the hearthed fireplace. The galley-style kitchen features a pantry, a bump-out window over the sink, and easy access to the combined laundry/tility room. The breakfast nook, which overlooks the deck, is flooded with light from the uniquely arranged windows. The three bedrooms and two baths are on the other side of the core of activity rooms. The master bedroom has a private bath plus a double vanity, walk-in and a walk-in closet in the dressing area.

First floor — 1,737 sq. ft.
Basement — 1,737 sq. ft.
Garage — 584 sq. ft.

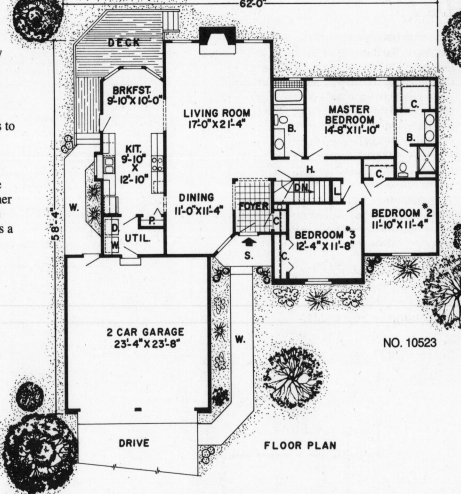

DECK

BRKFST.
9'-10" X 10'-0"

LIVING ROOM
17'-0" X 21'-4"

MASTER BEDROOM
14'-8" X 11'-10"

KIT.
9'-10" X 12'-10"

DINING
11'-0" X 11'-4"

FOYER

H.

BEDROOM 2
11'-10" X 11'-4"

W.

D
W

UTIL.

P.

BEDROOM 3
12'-4" X 11'-8"

S.

C.

62'-0"

58'-4"

2 CAR GARAGE
23'-4" X 23'-8"

W.

NO. 10523

DRIVE

FLOOR PLAN

A Karl Kreeger Design

Zoned for Privacy

No. 91217

Don't worry about compromising your privacy in this one-level beauty. This plan is zoned to keep active and quiet areas separate. Step down from the foyer to a wide-open living room that flows into the formal dining room. Cathedral ceilings add to the spacious feeling that continues throughout active areas with an island kitchen open to the breakfast room. French doors lead from the kitchen to a screened porch, a nice warm-weather spot for your morning coffee. Down a hallway off the living room lie three bedrooms, each with a unique character. Notice how closets provide a separation from the bustle of active areas. And, with two full baths, even the morning rush shouldn't be a problem in this house.

Living area — 1,811 sq. ft.
Screened porch — 121 sq. ft.
Garage — 437 sq. ft.

No materials list available

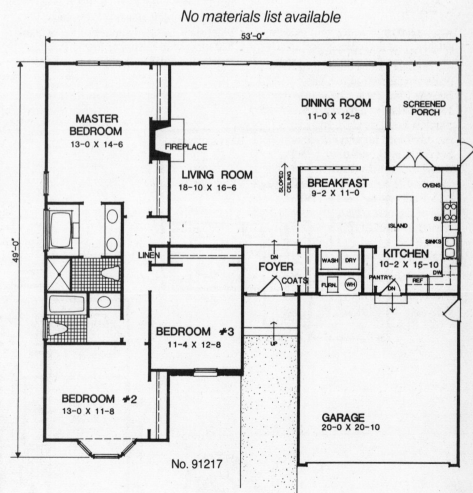

No. 91217

Sheltered Porch is an Inviting Entrance

No. 20070

Traditional design unites with modern, open spaces in this compact colonial. Featuring a dramatic two story entry, bay windows in the fireplaced living and breakfast nook brighten the first floor. The dining room, kitchen, half bath, and utility room with access to the two car garage complete this level. Upstairs, a plant shelf takes advantage of the octagonal window in the upper foyer. Two bedrooms and a full bath share the second floor with a large master bedroom suite highlighted by a skylit bath with separate shower and tub, double vanity, and ample closet space.

First floor — 877 sq. ft.
Second floor — 910 sq. ft.
Basement — 877 sq. ft.
Garage — 458 sq. ft.

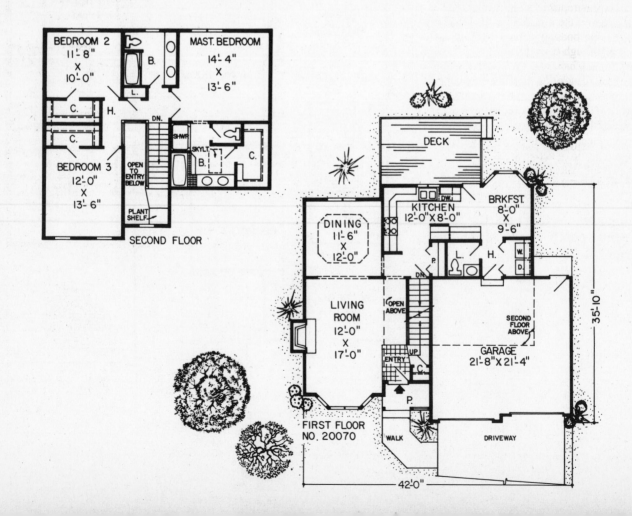

Foyer Isolates Bedroom Wing

No. 20087

Don't worry about waking up the kids. They'll sleep soundly in a quiet atmosphere away from main living areas, on a hallway off the foyer of this charming one-level. Sunny and open, the living room features a window-wall flanking a massive fireplace, and access to a deck at the rear of the house. The adjoining dining room boasts recessed ceilings, and pass-through convenience to the kitchen and breakfast room. You'll find the master suite, tucked behind the two-car garage for maximum quiet, a pleasant retreat that includes double vanities, a walk-in closet, and both shower and tub.

First floor — 1,568 sq. ft.
Bsement — 1,568 sq. ft.
Garage — 484 sq. ft.

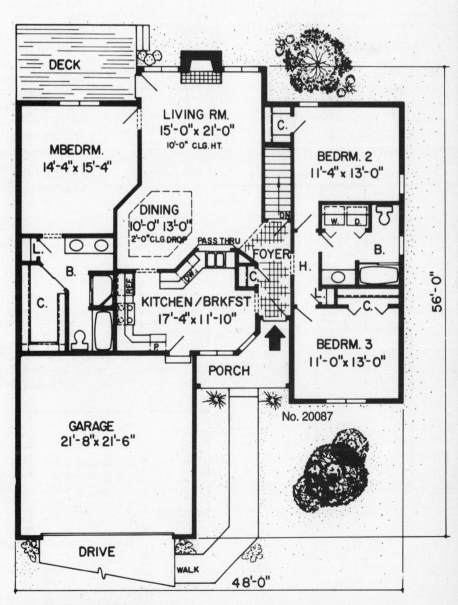

DECK

LIVING RM.
15'-0" x 21'-0"
10'-0" CLG. HT.

MBEDRM.
14'-4" x 15'-4"

C.

BEDRM. 2
11'-4" x 13'-0"

DINING
10'-0" 13'-0"
2'-0" CLG. DROP

W. D.

B.

PASS THRU

FOYER

B.

C.

H.

C.

KITCHEN/BRKFST
17'-4" x 11'-10"

DN

C.

BEDRM. 3
11'-0" x 13'-0"

PORCH

No. 20087

GARAGE
21'-8" x 21'-6"

56'-0"

DRIVE

WALK

48'-0"

A Karl Kreeger Design

Window Boxes Add Romantic Charm

No. 90684

Practical yet pretty, this ranch home separates active and quiet areas for privacy when you want it. To the left, off the central foyer, you'll find a formal living and dining room combination that's just perfect for entertaining. The wing to the right of the foyer includes three spacious bedrooms and two full baths. Sunlight and warmth pervade the open, informal areas at the rear of the house, where the kitchen, dining bay, and family room enjoy the benefits of a large fireplace and an expansive glass wall overlooking the patio. When the kids come home after a day's play, you'll appreciate the convenient lavatory location just inside the back door. There's plenty of storage space in the garage, just past the mudroom off the kitchen.

Living area — 1,486 sq. ft.
Garage — 2-car

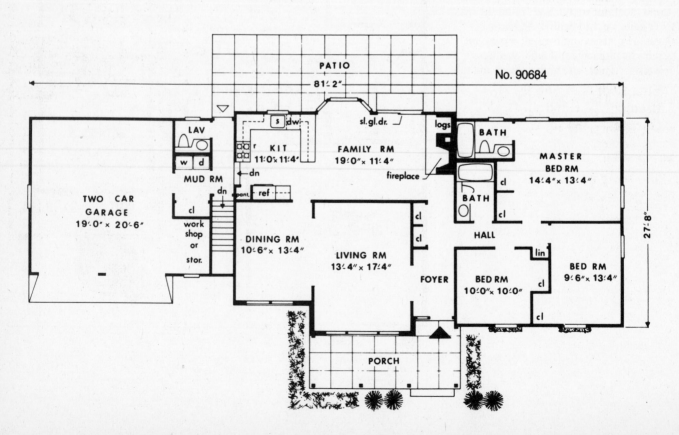

Interior and Exterior Unity Distinguishes Plan

No. 90398

Are you a sun worshipper? A rear orientation and a huge, wrap-around deck make this one-level home an outdoor lover's dream. Stepping into the entry, you're afforded a panoramic view of active areas from the exciting vaulted living room to the angular kitchen overlooking the cheerful breakfast nook. Columns divide the living and dining rooms. Half-walls separate the kitchen and breakfast room. And, the result is a sunny celebration of open space not often found in a one-level home. Bedrooms feature special window treatments and interesting angles. A full bath serves the two front bedrooms, but the luxurious master suite boasts its own private, skylit bath with double vanities, as well as a generous walk-in closet.

Main living area — 1,630 sq. ft.
Garage — 2-car

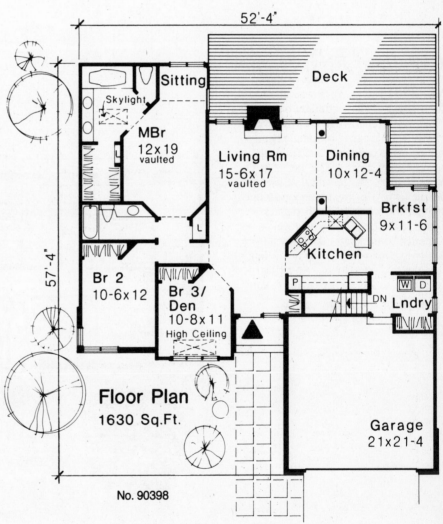

52'-4"

57'-4"

Sitting

Skylight

MBr
12 x 19
vaulted

Deck

Living Rm
15-6 x 17
vaulted

Dining
10 x 12-4

Brkfst
9 x 11-6

Kitchen

Br 2
10-6 x 12

Br 3/
Den
10-8 x 11
High Ceiling

P

W D
DN
Lndry

Floor Plan
1630 Sq.Ft.

Garage
21 x 21-4

No. 90398

SOLAR HOME

Excellent First Home

No. 28015

Solar storage cells on the south side contribute to the energy-saving effectiveness of this well-designed beginning family home. Three bedrooms and two baths occupy the east wing. The master bedroom features a large walk-in closet and private bath. The great room opens out onto a patio while the kitchen gives access to the large double garage. A breakfast bar separates the kitchen from the living area while giving the feeling of spacious and open living. An air-lock entry adds to the energy-saving features.

**First floor — 1,296 sq. ft.
Garage — 484 sq. ft.**

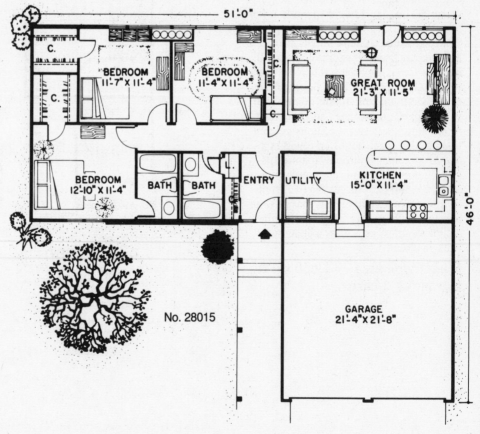

51'-0"
46'-0"

C.
C.
C.

BEDROOM
11'-7" X 11'-4"

BEDROOM
11'-4" X 11'-4"

C.
C.

GREAT ROOM
21'-3" X 11'-5"

BEDROOM
12'-10" X 11'-4"

BATH
BATH
ENTRY
UTILITY

KITCHEN
15'-0" X 11'-4"

No. 28015

GARAGE
21'-4" X 21'-8"

Floor Plan Accents
Open Design

No. 90304

A second floor study opens onto the living room below to give the feeling of extra spaciousness. Behind the living room, the family room opens onto the patio and the adjacent kitchen to further the design concept. The U-shaped kitchen offers plenty of storage and a high degree of efficiency plus lots of light provided by its own set of windows onto the patio. The main floor incorporates one bedroom with double closets and a full bath plus linen closet. The second floor makes storage and also allows for the other bedroom and its full-sized bath.

Total area — 1,410 sq. ft.

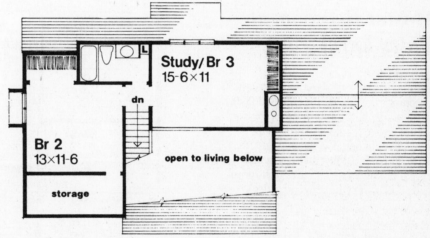

Study/Br 3
15-6 × 11

Br 2
13 × 11-6

dn

open to living below

storage

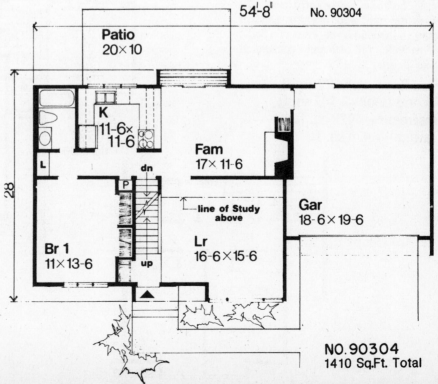

54-8" No. 90304

Patio
20 × 10

K
11-6×
11-6

Fam
17 × 11-6

28

P

dn

line of Study above

Gar
18-6 × 19-6

Br 1
11 × 13-6

up

Lr
16-6 × 15-6

NO. 90304
1410 Sq.Ft. Total

Master Bedroom at Entry Level

No. 20060

Striking angles best describes this contemporary design. At the front entrance, an attractive half-circle window transom is built above the door. Through the foyer, the kitchen is centered perfectly between the breakfast area and a more formal dining area. The breakfast room leads onto a very large wooden deck through sliding glass doors. From the breakfast room, the living room comes complete with a burning fireplace, plus the extra feature of a sloping, open beamed ceiling. This design offers the master bedroom on the entry level, with a dressing area, walk-in closet, and full bath. The second level offers two bedrooms with a full bath and a convenient cedar closet.

First floor — 1,279 sq. ft.
Second floor — 502 sq. ft.
Basement — 729 sq. ft.
Garage — 470 sq. ft.

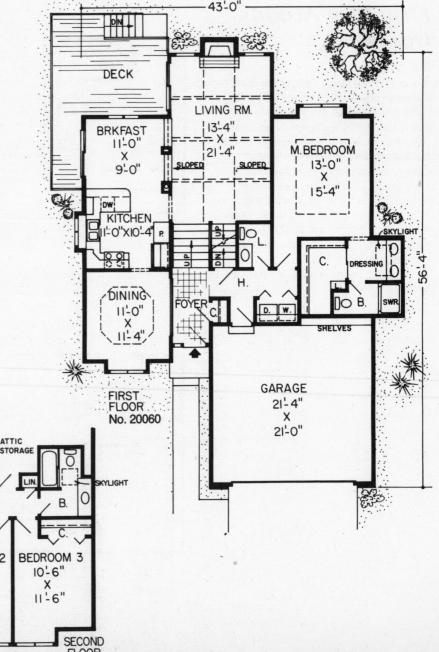

Carefree Living on One Level

No. 20089

Here's an inviting little charmer that will keep housework to a minimum and give you plenty of room for hobbies. A full basement and oversized two-car garage is large enough to store your cars and boat, with space left for a workshop. Upstairs,

one-level living is a breeze in this plan that keeps active and quiet areas separate. Three bedrooms and two full baths tucked down a hallway include the spacious master suite with double vanities. The fireplaced living room, dining room, and kitchen are wide open and conveniently arranged for easy mealtimes.

Take it easy after dinner, and enjoy dessert and coffee outside on the deck off the dining room.

Main living area — 1,588 sq. ft.
Basement — 780 sq. ft.
Garage — 808 sq. ft.

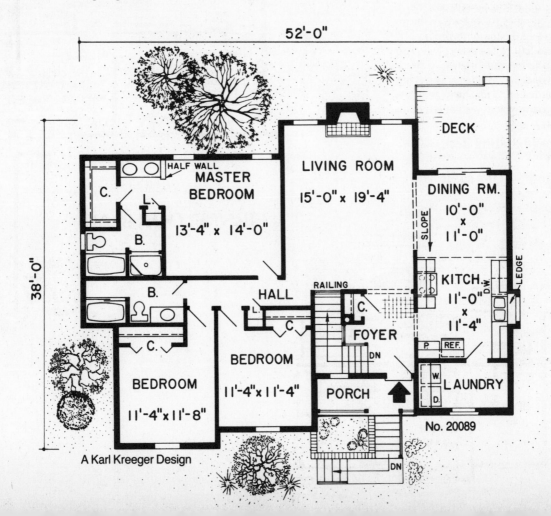

A Karl Kreeger Design

Designed for the TV Buff

No. 90621

No matter where you decide to build, you'll be sure to get perfect TV reception in the living room of this passive solar home. A satellite dish shares south-facing roof space with skylights and hot water solar collectors. And, the entertainment center is visible from all the living areas, grouped together in one, open space. The entrance foyer leads to the main rooms and the master bedroom off the bathroom hall. The upstairs hall, two bedrooms, and bath are brightened by clerestory windows. With energy-saving construction features, this home will give you years of enjoyment with minimal energy costs.

First floor (exluding deck) — 967 sq. ft.
Second floor — 389 sq. ft.

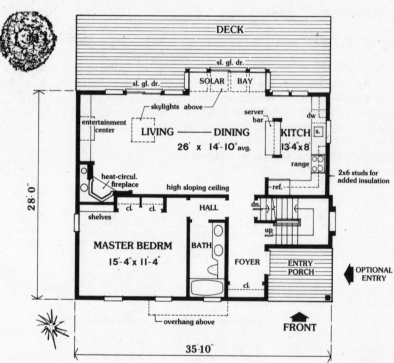

FIRST FLOOR PLAN

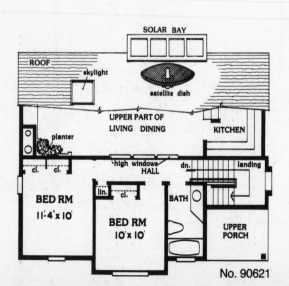

No. 90621

Rustic Vacation House

No. 90004

This compact three-bedroom cabin, designed for vacations and later retirement, would suit many areas. The stone and wood exterior requires little maintenance. Two porches and an outdoor balcony make the most of entertaining, relaxing, or just enjoying a sunset. From the foyer, the spiral stairway in the living room can be seen which leads to a balcony and an upstairs bedroom or studio. A wood fire always seems to make a house warmer and cozier, and this design includes a massive stone fireplace in the living room. The living room also has a pair of floor-to-ceiling windows at the gable end and sliding glass doors to a rear porch. There is a pantry adjoining the eat-in kitchen which has a small bay window over the sink. Off the foyer is a powder room. The design also includes two bedrooms and a bath on the first floor.

First floor — 1,020 sq. ft.
Second floor — 265 sq. ft.

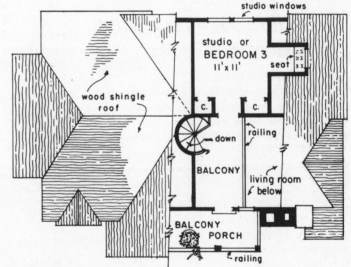

balcony level   No. 90004

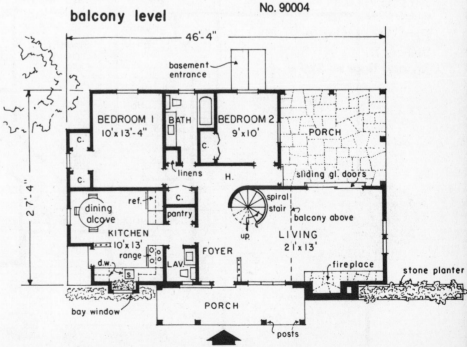

first floor

Railing Divides Living Spaces

No. 10596
This one-level design is a celebration of light and open space. From the foyer, view the dining room, island kitchen, breakfast room, living room, and outdoor deck in one sweeping glance. Bay windows add pleasing angles and lots of sunshine to eating areas and the master suite. And, a wall of windows brings the outdoors into the two back bedrooms.

Upper floor — 1,740 sq. ft.
Basement — 1,377 sq. ft.
Garage — 480 sq. ft.

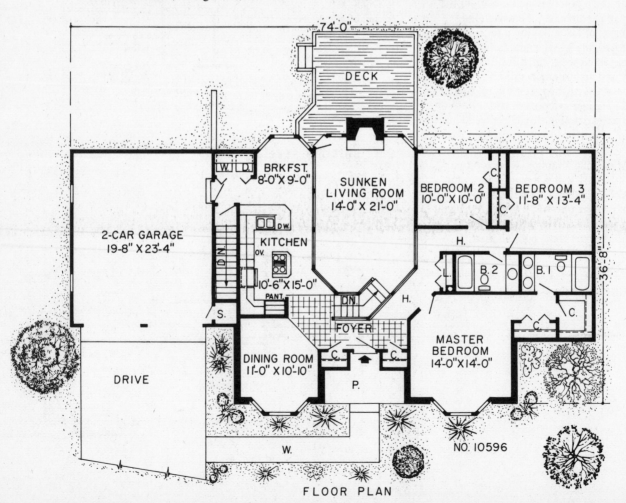

FLOOR PLAN

Half-Round Window Graces Attractive Exterior

No. 90395

This handsome home combines convenience and drama by adding a bedroom wing a half-level above active areas. The result of this distinctive design is a strik- ing, spacious feeling in living spaces, along with uncompromised privacy for the two bedrooms at the rear of the house. Look at the soaring ceilings of the kitchen, living, dining, and breakfast rooms. Notice the little touches that make life easier: the private bath entrance from the master suite, the pass-through between kitchen and dining room, the built-in planning desk, the bookcases that flank the fireplace. Don't need a third bedroom? The front room on the entry level doubles as a home office or den.

Main living area — 1,452 sq. ft.
Garage — 2-car

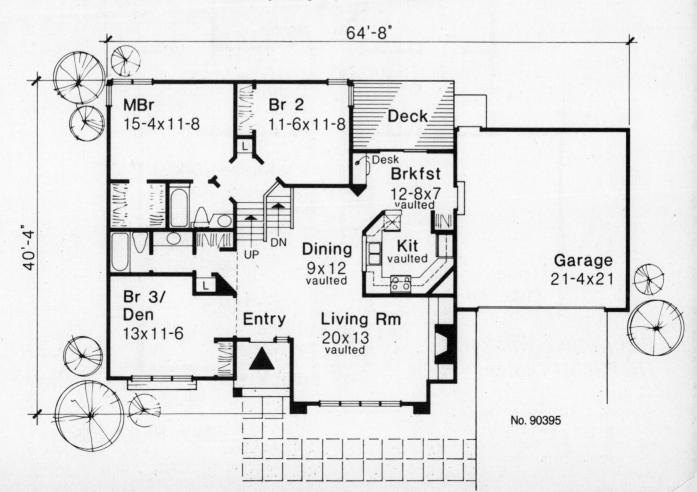

No. 90395

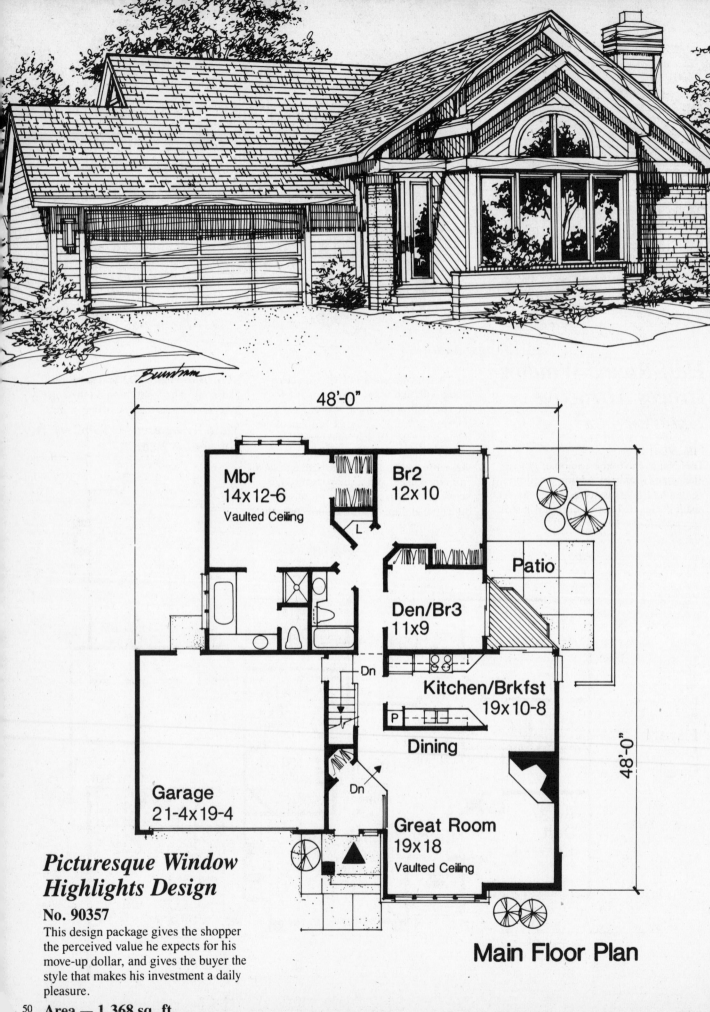

48'-0"

Mbr
14x12-6
Vaulted Ceiling

Br2
12x10

Patio

Den/Br3
11x9

L

Dn

Kitchen/Brkfst
19x10-8

P

Dining

Garage
21-4x19-4

Dn

Great Room
19x18
Vaulted Ceiling

48'-0"

Picturesque Window Highlights Design

No. 90357

This design package gives the shopper the perceived value he expects for his move-up dollar, and gives the buyer the style that makes his investment a daily pleasure.

Main Floor Plan

Area — 1,368 sq. ft.

Compact Classic

No. 91413

Designed with economy in mind, this traditional treasure will give you a lot of house for your building dollar. And, its compact shape and attractive Colonial exterior make this home an asset to any neighborhood. The main floor is divided into formal and family areas. Entertain in the living and dining rooms, separated by the L-shaped, open staircase to the second floor. The powder room around the corner means guests don't have to walk upstairs. You'll enjoy the view from the rear of the house, where the kitchen, nook, and family room flow together for a wide-open feeling accentuated by lots of windows and an atrium door to the patio. Upstairs, three bedrooms and two full baths include the spacious master suite.

First floor — 963 sq. ft.
Second floor — 774 sq. ft.
Garage — 2-car

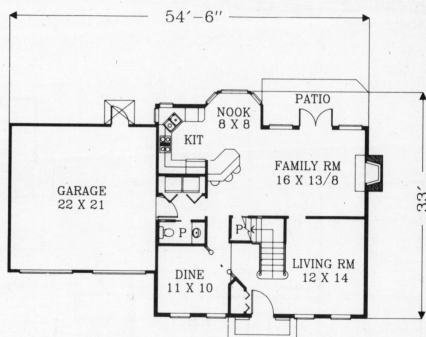

FIRST FLOOR PLAN

No. 91413

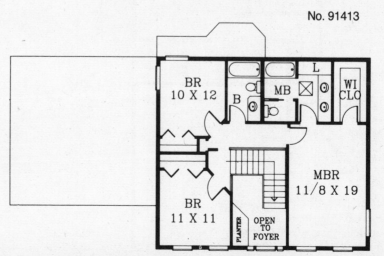

SECOND FLOOR PLAN

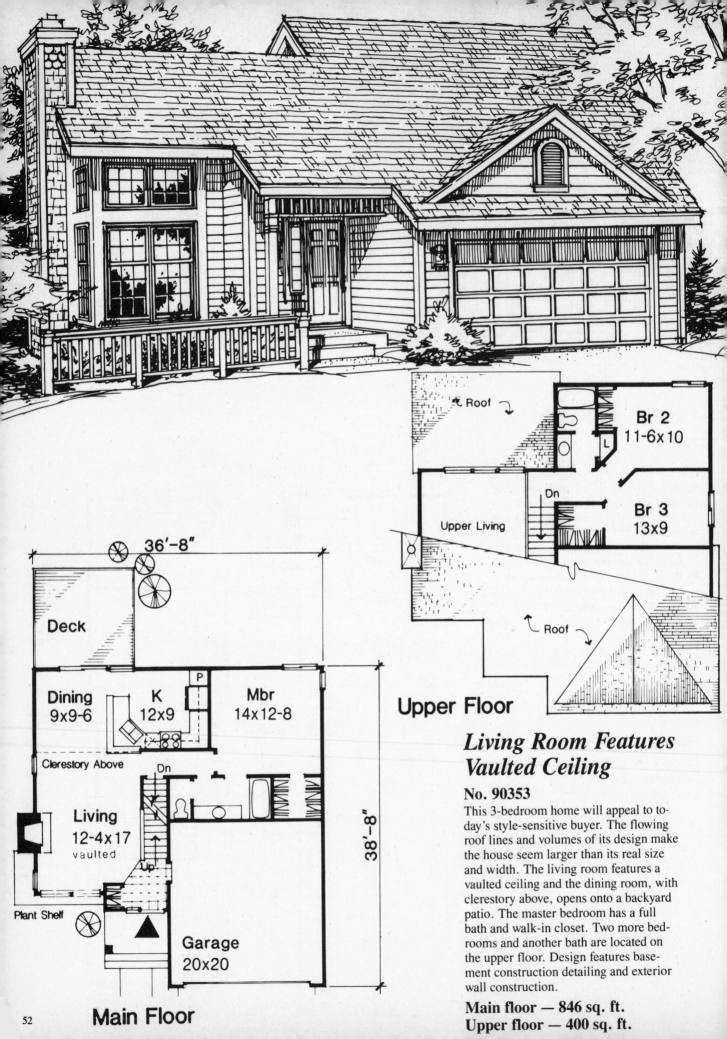

Upper Floor

Br 2
11-6x10

Dn

Br 3
13x9

Upper Living

Roof

Roof

Main Floor

36'-8"

Deck

Dining
9x9-6

K
12x9

P

Mbr
14x12-8

Clerestory Above

Dn

Living
12-4x17
vaulted

Up

Plant Shelf

Garage
20x20

38'-8"

Living Room Features Vaulted Ceiling

No. 90353

This 3-bedroom home will appeal to today's style-sensitive buyer. The flowing roof lines and volumes of its design make the house seem larger than its real size and width. The living room features a vaulted ceiling and the dining room, with clerestory above, opens onto a backyard patio. The master bedroom has a full bath and walk-in closet. Two more bedrooms and another bath are located on the upper floor. Design features basement construction detailing and exterior wall construction.

Main floor — 846 sq. ft.
Upper floor — 400 sq. ft.

52

Dutch Colonial Accent

No. 90686

Face the rear of this one-level home south to take advantage of the warmth and light you'll gain through its abundant windows and sliding glass doors. Its sunny atmosphere is accentuated by a greenhouse bay in the dining room, and a skylight piercing the soaring ceiling of the spacious living room. You'll appreciate the central kitchen location whether you're serving a formal dinner, a barbecue on the terrace, or popcorn in the family room. A hallway off the foyer leads past a full bath to three bedrooms. The rear-facing master suite includes a walk-in closet and private bath with double vanities and a whirlpool tub. Build this home with or without a basement; there's lots of storage space in the garage.

Main living area — 1,544 sq. ft.
Laundry-mud room — 74 sq. ft.
Garage-storage — 516 sq. ft.

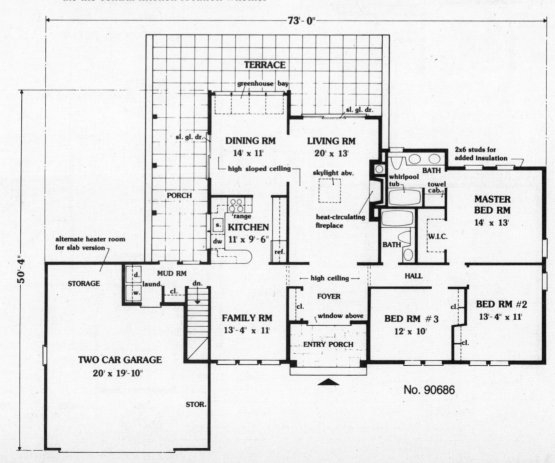

No. 90686

Stucco and Stone Reveal Outstanding Tudor Design

No. 10555

This beautiful stucco and stone masonry Tudor design opens to a formal foyer that leads through double doors into a well-designed library which is also conve- niently accessible from the master bed- room. The master bedroom offers a vaulted ceiling and a huge bath area. Other features are an oversized living room with a fireplace, an open kitchen and a connecting dining room. A utility room and half bath are located next to a two-car garage. One other select option in this design is the separate cedar closet to use for off-season clothes storage.

First floor — 1,671 sq. ft.
Second floor — 505 sq. ft.
Basement — 1,661 sq. ft.
Garage — 604 sq. ft.
Screened porch — 114 sq. ft.

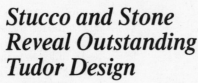

BEDROOM
11'-8" X 9'-10"

CEDAR CLOS.

C.

C. L.

B.

BEDROOM
11'-8" X 13'-2"

BALCONY

DN.

FOYER BELOW

SECOND FLOOR

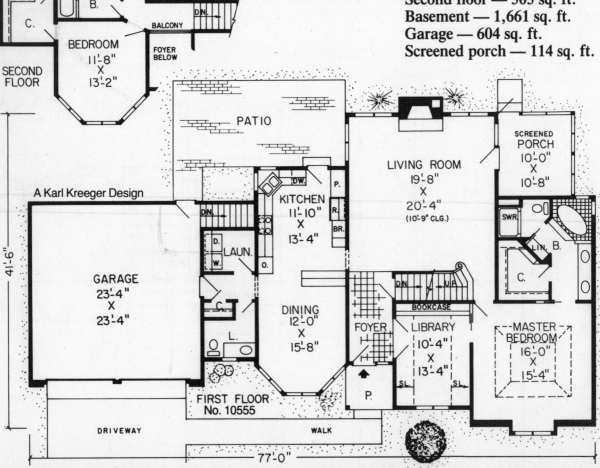

PATIO

A Karl Kreeger Design

GARAGE
23'-4" X 23'-4"

DN.

D. W. LAUN.

C.

L.

KITCHEN
11'-10" X 13'-4"

DW.

P.

R.

BR.

O.

DINING
12'-0" X 15'-8"

LIVING ROOM
19'-8" X 20'-4"
(10'-9" CLG.)

SCREENED PORCH
10'-0" X 10'-8"

SWR

LIN. B.

C.

DN. UP

BOOKCASE

FOYER

LIBRARY
10'-4" X 13'-4"

SL SL

MASTER BEDROOM
16'-0" X 15'-4"

P.

FIRST FLOOR
No. 10555

DRIVEWAY

WALK

41'-6"

77'-0"

Ranch Style Favors Living Room

No. 6360

Stretching over 22 feet to span the width of this ranch design, the living room is indulged with expanses of windows, a wood-burning fireplace, and access to the terrace. A separate, well-windowed din-ing room and an efficient kitchen with abundant counter space border the living room. Three bedrooms complete this plan.

Main floor — 1,342 sq.ft.
Basement — 767 sq.ft.
Garage — 466 sq.ft.
Terrace — 92 sq.ft.

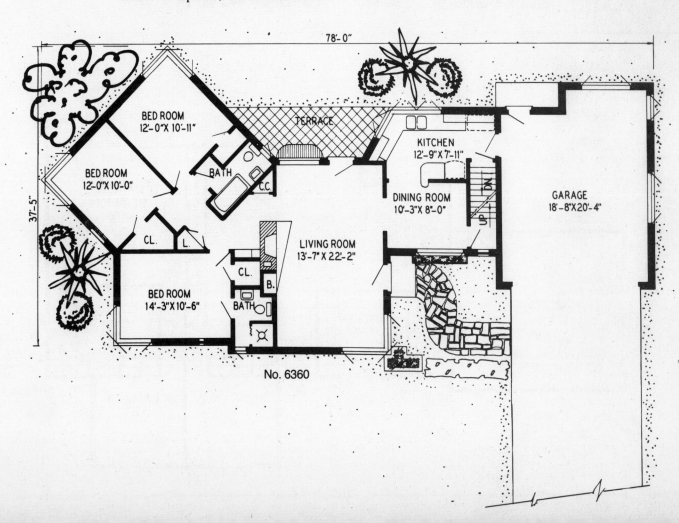

No. 6360

Beamed Ceiling and Corner Fireplace Add Unusual Accents

No. 10506

This home's spacious living room will be enjoyed by guests and family alike. In addition to the beamed ceiling and corner fireplace, it opens onto a large, angled deck and has its own wet bar.

The living room also adjoins the dining room and shares an eating bar with the kitchen. This well designed kitchen provides plenty of work space and storage plus room for extra cooks. The three bedrooms complete the floor plan. The master bedroom has a full-wall closet, five-piece bath plus direct access to the deck through sliding glass doors.

**First floor — 1,893 sq. ft.
Garage — 494 sq. ft.**

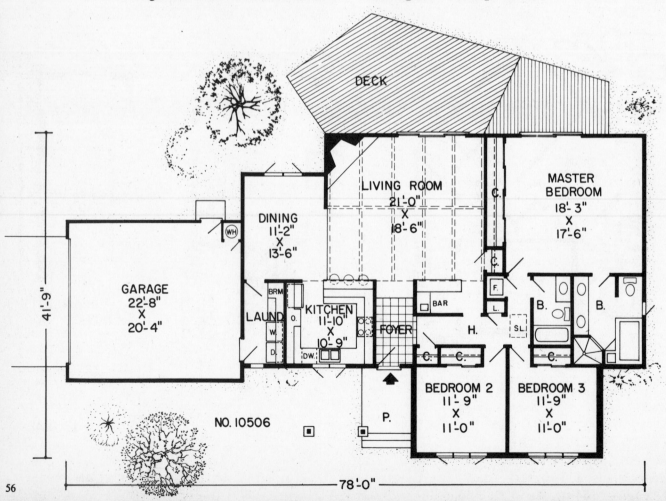

DECK

LIVING ROOM
21'-0"
X
18'-6"

MASTER BEDROOM
18'-3"
X
17'-6"

DINING
11'-2"
X
13'-6"

GARAGE
22'-8"
X
20'-4"

BRM

LAUND

KITCHEN
11'-10"
X
10'-9"

BAR

FOYER

BEDROOM 2
11'-9"
X
11'-0"

BEDROOM 3
11'-9"
X
11'-0"

41'-9"

78'-0"

NO. 10506

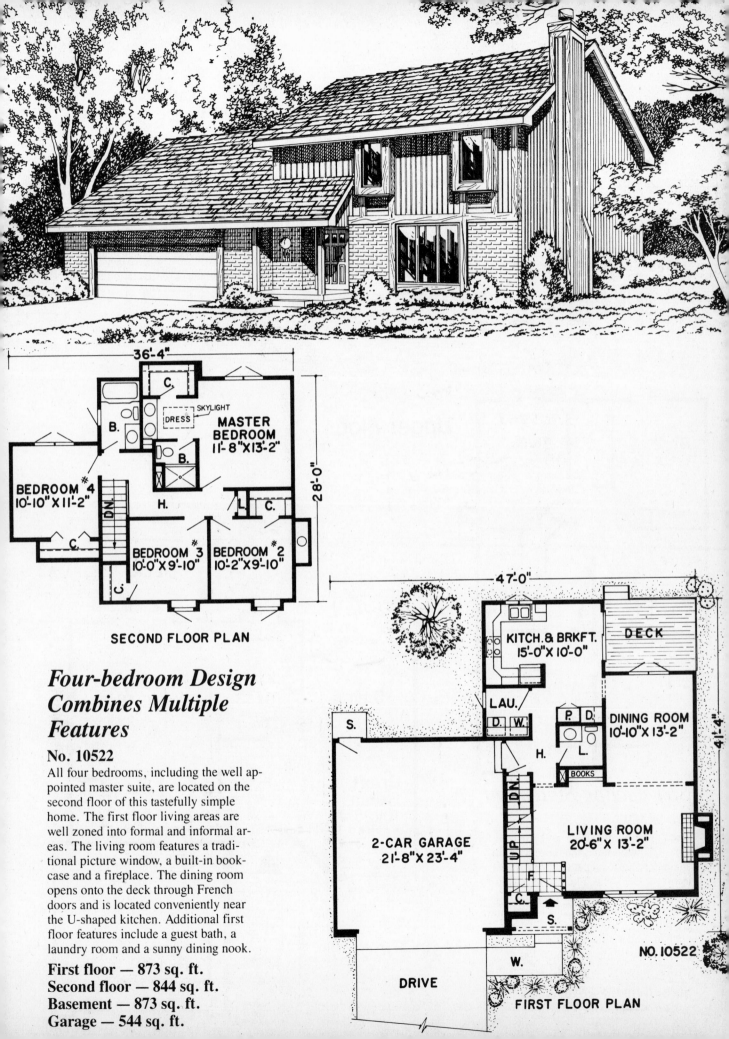

SECOND FLOOR PLAN

36'-4"

C

SKYLIGHT

DRESS

MASTER BEDROOM 11'-8" X 13'-2"

B.

B.

H.

L.

C.

BEDROOM #4 10'-10" X 11'-2"

DN

C.

BEDROOM #3 10'-0" X 9'-10"

BEDROOM #2 10'-2" X 9'-10"

C.

28'-0"

Four-bedroom Design Combines Multiple Features

No. 10522

All four bedrooms, including the well appointed master suite, are located on the second floor of this tastefully simple home. The first floor living areas are well zoned into formal and informal areas. The living room features a traditional picture window, a built-in bookcase and a fireplace. The dining room opens onto the deck through French doors and is located conveniently near the U-shaped kitchen. Additional first floor features include a guest bath, a laundry room and a sunny dining nook.

First floor — 873 sq. ft.
Second floor — 844 sq. ft.
Basement — 873 sq. ft.
Garage — 544 sq. ft.

47'-0"

KITCH. & BRKFT. 15'-0" X 10'-0"

DECK

LAU.

P. D.

D. W.

DINING ROOM 10'-10" X 13'-2"

S.

H.

L.

BOOKS

DN

2-CAR GARAGE 21'-8" X 23'-4"

UP

LIVING ROOM 20'-6" X 13'-2"

F.

C.

S.

W.

41'-4"

NO. 10522

DRIVE

FIRST FLOOR PLAN

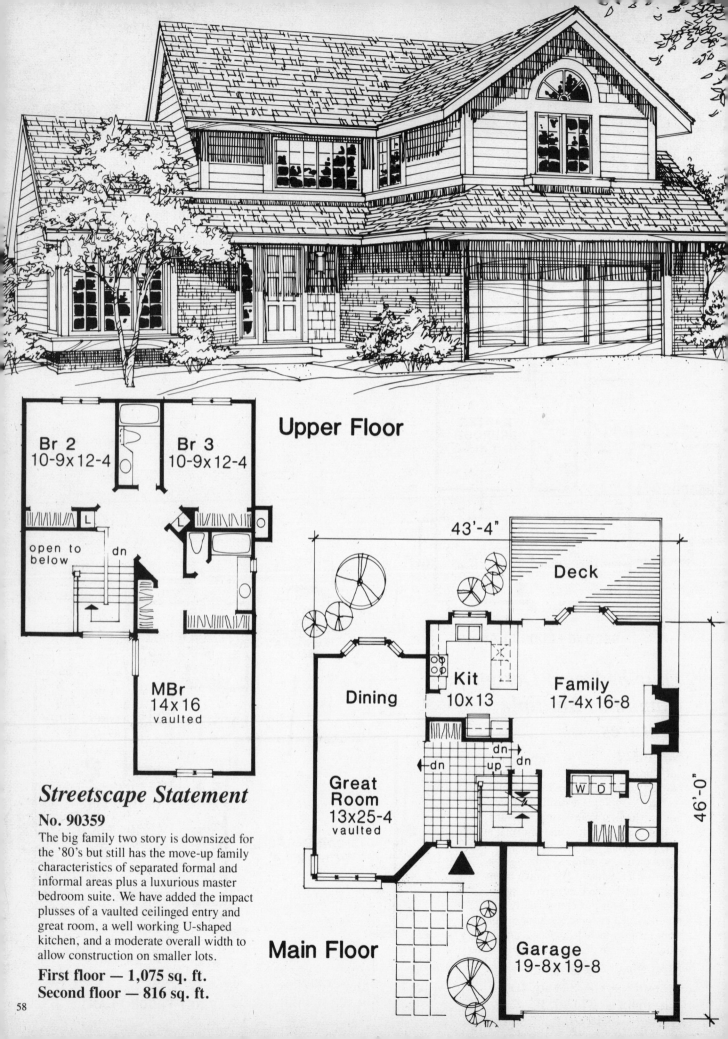

Upper Floor

Br 2
10-9x12-4

Br 3
10-9x12-4

open to
below

dn

MBr
14x16
vaulted

Streetscape Statement

No. 90359

The big family two story is downsized for the '80's but still has the move-up family characteristics of separated formal and informal areas plus a luxurious master bedroom suite. We have added the impact plusses of a vaulted ceilinged entry and great room, a well working U-shaped kitchen, and a moderate overall width to allow construction on smaller lots.

First floor — 1,075 sq. ft.
Second floor — 816 sq. ft.

43'-4"

Deck

Dining

Kit
10x13

Family
17-4x16-8

46'-0"

dn

up

dn

dn

W D

Great
Room
13x25-4
vaulted

Garage
19-8x19-8

Main Floor

Overhang Provides Shade from the Noonday Sun

No. 90502

A sheltered entry opens to the airy, fire-placed living and dining room of this one-level, stucco home. Behind double doors, the family room shares a view of the deck with the kitchen and adjoining, bay windowed breakfast nook. The window of the front bedroom, framed by a graceful arch, looks out over its own, private garden. An angular hall leads to the laundry, two additional bedrooms and two full baths.

Floor area — 1,642 sq. ft.

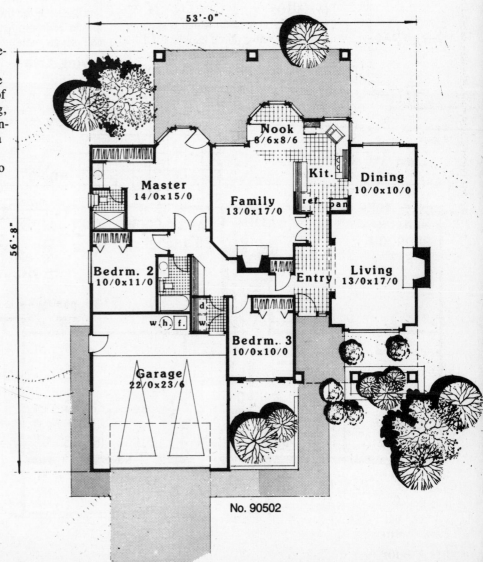

53'-0"

56'-8"

Nook
8/6x8/6

Master
14/0x15/0

Kit.

Dining
10/0x10/0

Family
13/0x17/0

ref. pan.

Bedrm. 2
10/0x11/0

Living
13/0x17/0

Entry

w. h. f.
d
w

Bedrm. 3
10/0x10/0

Garage
22/0x23/6

No. 90502

Graceful Porch Enhances Charm

No. 90106

The formal living room which is sheltered by the railed porch may be used only for company because of the multi-functional kitchen, dining and family room which are immediately behind it. This "three rooms in one" design is eas-ily adaptable to any number of lifestyles. Adjacent to the open kitchen with its efficient design and ample counter space is the hobby area that includes laundry facilities. Of the three large bedrooms the master bedroom features a walk-in closet and private bath.

Living Area — 1,643 sq. ft.

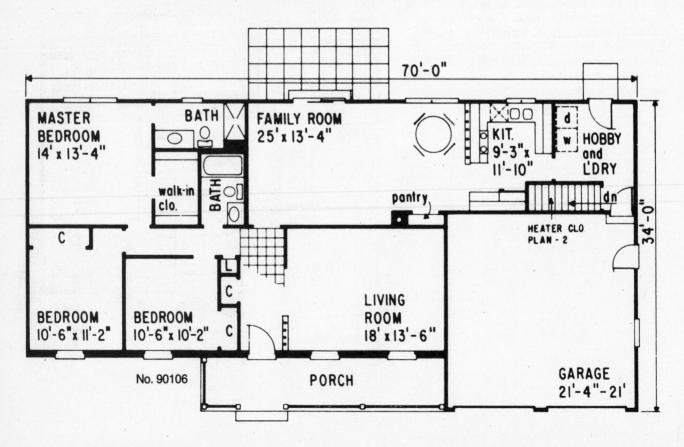

MASTER BEDROOM 14' x 13'-4"

BATH

FAMILY ROOM 25' x 13'-4"

KIT. 9'-3" x 11'-10"

HOBBY and L'DRY

walk-in clo.

BATH

pantry

HEATER CLO. PLAN - 2

BEDROOM 10'-6" x 11'-2"

BEDROOM 10'-6" x 10'-2"

LIVING ROOM 18' x 13'-6"

No. 90106

PORCH

GARAGE 21'-4" - 21'

70'-0"

34'-0"

High Impact in a Small Package

No. 19491

From the sheltered veranda to the connected active areas, this award-winning home says "welcome." Look at the efficient U-shaped kitchen, with pass-through convenience that keeps the cook in the conversation around the dining table. Ceilings soar to dramatic heights in the adjoining living room. And, upstairs, the master loft with its own private deck provides a commanding view of the scene below, along with loads of built-in storage. With its own private bath and room-sized closet, this room will be a retreat you'll never want to leave. Tucked away from active areas, a roomy first-floor bedroom and study flank a combined bath and laundry center.

First floor — 920 sq. ft.
Second floor — 300 sq. ft.
Garage — 583 sq. ft.

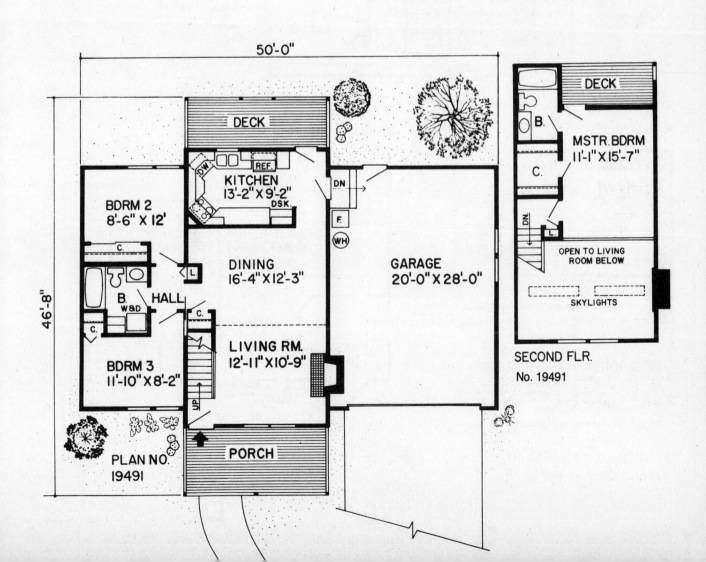

PLAN NO. 19491

SECOND FLR.
No. 19491

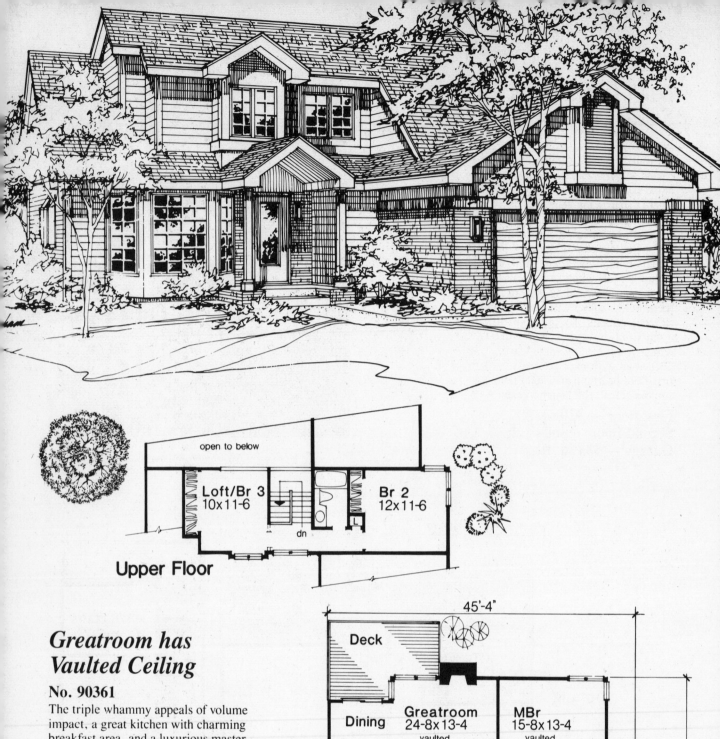

Upper Floor

Loft/Br 3
10x11-6

Br 2
12x11-6

open to below

dn

Greatroom has Vaulted Ceiling

No. 90361

The triple whammy appeals of volume impact, a great kitchen with charming breakfast area, and a luxurious master bedroom suite give this house lots of perceived value in today's very competitive mid-priced marketplace. Note how these features are emphasized with balconied stair overlooking living and dininjg rooms, greenhouse plus bay windowed kitchen, and master bath with platform tub plus stall shower plus oversized walk-in closet. Combined with the highly detailed, custom look exterior, this total design package gives your buyer a lot to like.

**First floor — 1,105 sq. ft.
Second floor — 460 sq. ft.**

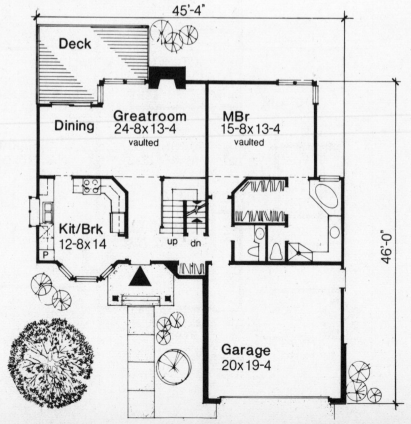

45'-4"

Deck

Dining

Greatroom
24-8x13-4
vaulted

MBr
15-8x13-4
vaulted

Kit/Brk
12-8x14

up   dn

46'-0"

Garage
20x19-4

Clapboard Classic

No. 90565

This tidy traditional packs a lot of living space into a small package. You'll love the sunny character of the open living and dining room arrangement that spans the entire width of the house. And, you'll find the same spacious feeling in the family room and adjoining dining bay off the kitchen. Notice the smart planning that tucks a planning desk and pantry under the central staircase. Four bedrooms upstairs lie off the balcony overlooking the foyer. A full bath with double vanities serves the kids' rooms. But, the master suite features its own private bath, as well as a room-size wardrobe and a cozy sitting area dominated by a beautiful, half-round window.

First floor — 1,020 sq. ft.
Second floor — 1,020 sq. ft.
Garage — 2-car

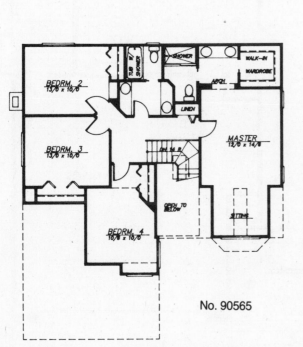

No. 90565

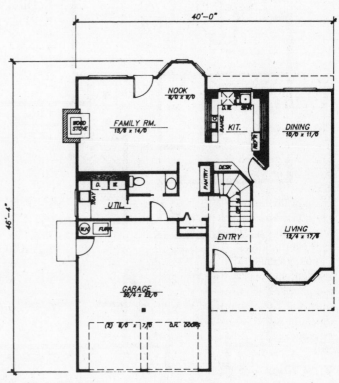

Striking Entryway

No. 20054

An expansive entrance with a cathedral ceiling in the living room offers a view of the entire house. The washer and dryer are located in the bedroom area, and even with small square footage, this home has a large master bedroom area and separate dining room and breakfast area. The deck is partially under the roof. The roof framing on this plan is simple, but the exterior is still interesting due to the large window and the farmhouse porch.

First floor — 1,461 sq. ft.
Basement — 1,435 sq. ft.
Garage — 528 sq. ft.

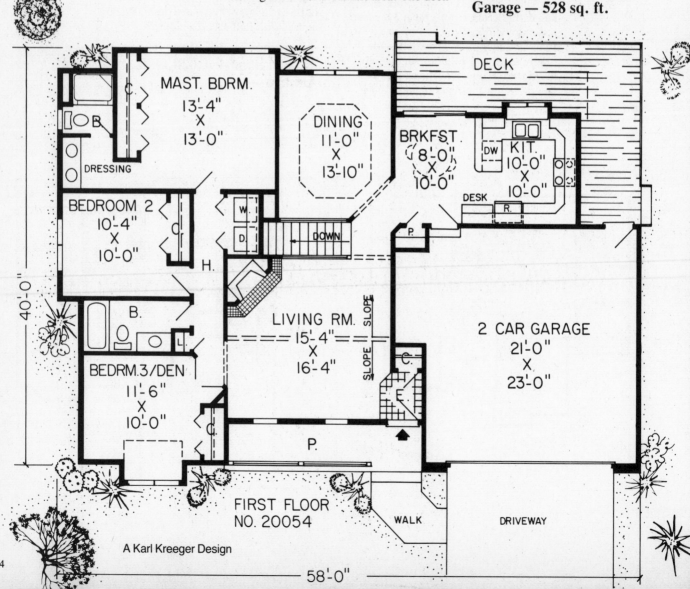

A Karl Kreeger Design

Plant Shelf Divides Living Space with Greenery

No. 90394

Twin gables, a beautiful half-round window, and Colonial-style corner boards give this one-story classic an inviting, traditional exterior that says "Welcome." Inside, the ingenious, open plan of active areas makes every room seem even larger. Look at the vaulted living room, where floor-to-ceiling windows flank the fireplace for a pleasing unity with the yard. In the spectacular dining room, which adjoins the kitchen for convenient mealtimes, sliding glass doors open to a rear deck. Three bedrooms at the rear of the house include the angular master suite, which features a private bath and double-sized closet.

Main living area — 1,252 sq. ft.
Garage — 2-car

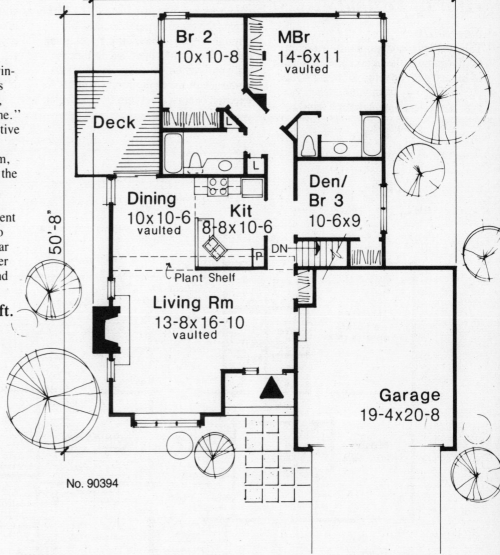

44'-8"

50'-8"

Br 2
10x10-8

MBr
14-6x11
vaulted

Deck

Den/
Br 3
10-6x9

Dining
10x10-6
vaulted

Kit
8-8x10-6

DN

Plant Shelf

Living Rm
13-8x16-10
vaulted

Garage
19-4x20-8

No. 90394

Easy Living, with a Hint of Drama

No. 90676

This one-level contemporary with a rustic, farmhouse flavor combines a touch of luxury with an informal plan. Watch the world go by from your kitchen vantage point, large enough for a family meal, and conveniently located for easy service to the formal dining room. When the weather's nice, use the built-in barbecue on the covered porch, accessible through sliders in both dining and living rooms. But, when there's a chill in the air, you'll enjoy the cozy, yet spacious ambience of the living room, with its exposed beams, crackling fire, and soaring, cathedral ceilings. You'll also appreciate the privacy of three bedrooms, down the hallway off the foyer. Hall and master baths feature convenient, split design and double-bowl vanities.

Living area — 1,575 sq. ft.
Garage — 2-car

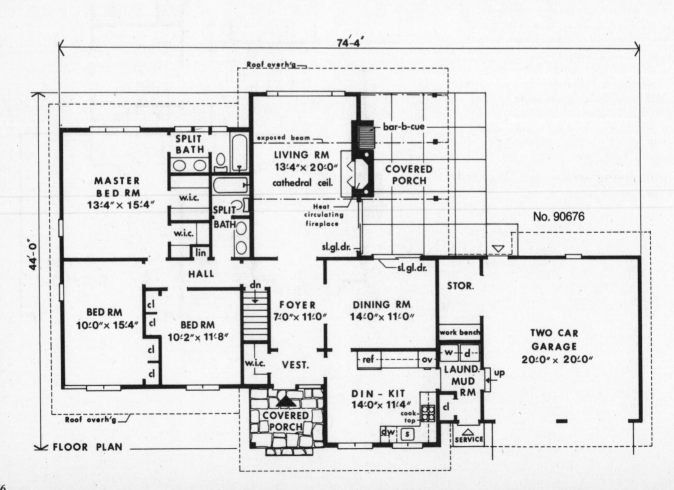

Comfortable Family Room in Congenial Setting

No. 90520

A secluded porch provides an intimate entrance to this 3 bedroom home. You'll appreciate the large family room with fireplace as the center for many activities. The breakfast nook will be popular with its nearby bow window and will be practible near the pantry and kitchen. The dining area also is easy to serve. The living room will have a wonderful view through the bow window. The master bedroom is complete, including dressing area and walk-in wardrobe.

First floor — 1,048 sq. ft.
Second floor — 726 sq. ft.

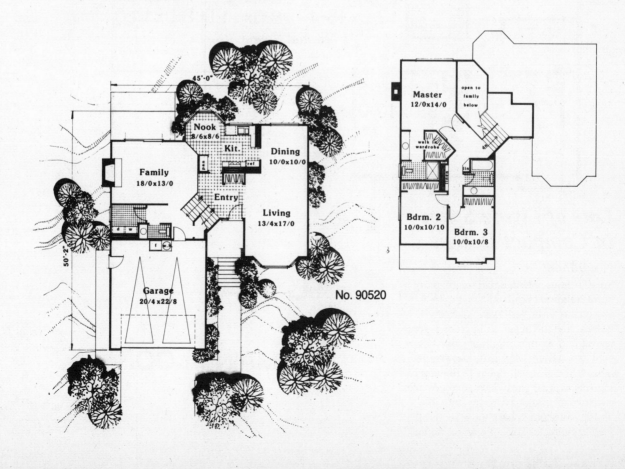

No. 90520

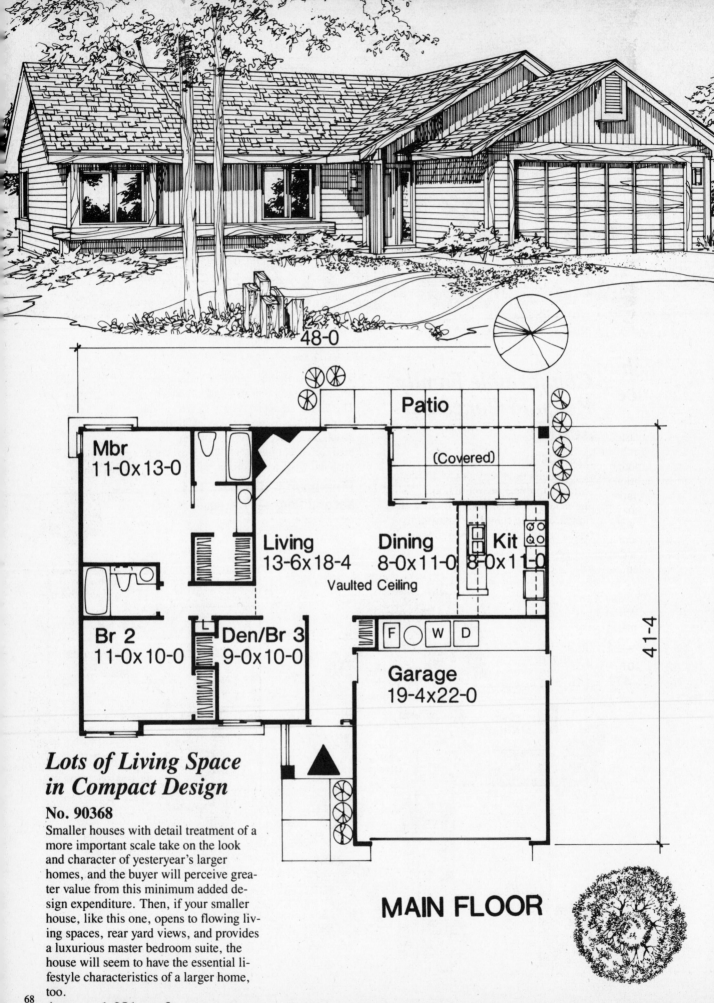

Patio

(Covered)

Mbr
11-0x13-0

Living
13-6x18-4

Dining
8-0x11-0

Kit
8-0x11-0

Vaulted Ceiling

Br 2
11-0x10-0

Den/Br 3
9-0x10-0

F W D

Garage
19-4x22-0

48-0

41-4

Lots of Living Space in Compact Design

No. 90368

Smaller houses with detail treatment of a more important scale take on the look and character of yesteryear's larger homes, and the buyer will perceive greater value from this minimum added design expenditure. Then, if your smaller house, like this one, opens to flowing living spaces, rear yard views, and provides a luxurious master bedroom suite, the house will seem to have the essential lifestyle characteristics of a larger home, too.

MAIN FLOOR

Area — 1,081 sq. ft.

A Touch of Classic Elegance

No. 20079

There's no wasted space in this compact home that combines the best of classic design and modern convenience. If you're a traditionalist, you'll love the half-round windows, clapboard and brick facade, and cozy fireplace. But, from the moment you walk past the portico, you'll find exciting contemporary touches: soaring ceilings, a dramatic balcony, a U-shaped kitchen, and wide-open living areas. Laundry facilities are conveniently adjacent to the downstairs bedrooms. You'll enjoy retreating upstairs to your very private master suite.

First floor — 1,200 sq. ft.
Second floor — 461 sq. ft.
Garage — 475 sq. ft.
Basement — 1,200 sq. ft.

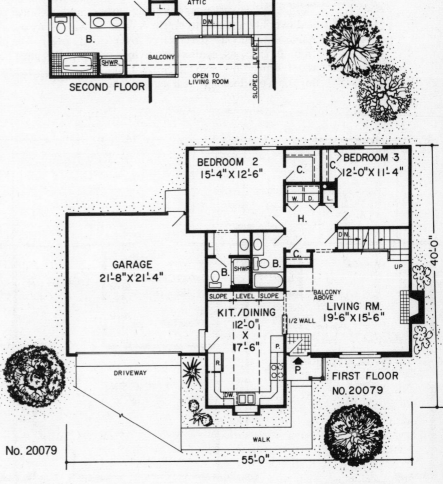

A Karl Kreeger Design

Expansive, Not Expensive

No. 90623

Despite its compact area, this home looks and lives like a luxurious ranch. A decorative screen divides the entrance foyer from the spacious, comfortable living room, which flows into the pleasant dining room overlooking a rear garden. The roomy, eat-in kitchen features a planning corner. And, the adjacent laundry-mud-room provides access to the two-car garage and to the outdoors. Here also lie the stairs to the full basement, a valuable, functional part of the house which adds many possibilities for informal family living. The private bedroom wing includes three bedrooms and two baths.

Total living area — 1,370 sq. ft.

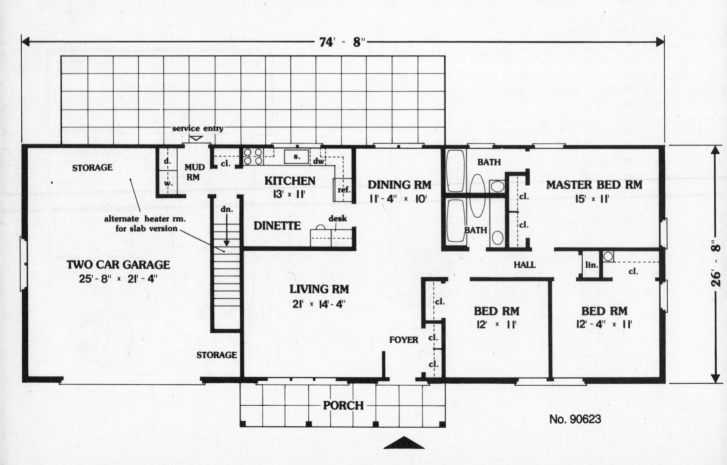

Extra Large Family Kitchen In Cozy Three Bedroom

No. 90134

The center of this three bedroom charmer is the extra large family kitchen. The galley-style food preparation area is located in one corner and separated from the rest of the room by a bar. Its placement near the carport entrance simplifies trips to the grocery store. Another convenience designed into this home is the placement of the laundry between the kitchen and the bedrooms. The three bedrooms are clustered around the full bath and one of the bedrooms features a private bath. In addition to the storage areas built into the living areas, a large outdoor storage closet is located at the back of the carport.

Living area — 1,120 sq. ft.

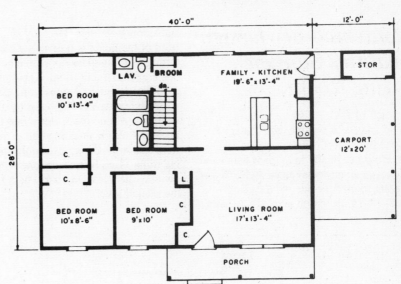

No. 90134   **WITH BASEMENT**

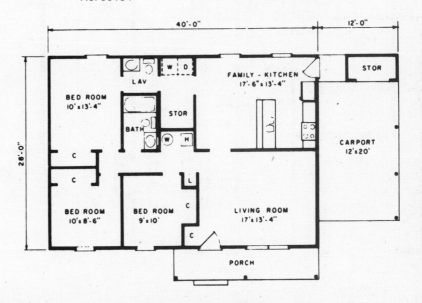

WITHOUT BASEMENT

Contemporary Design Features Sunken Living Room

No. 26112

Wood adds its warmth to the contemporary features of this passive solar design. Generous use of southern glass doors and windows, an air lock entry, skylights and a living room fireplace reduce energy needs. R-26 insulation is used for floors and sloping ceilings. Decking rims the front of the home and gives access through sliding glass doors to a bedroom/den area and living room. The dining room lies up several steps from the living room and is separated from it by a half wall. The dining room flows into the kitchen through an eating bar. A second floor landing balcony overlooks the living room. Two bedrooms, one with its own private deck, and a full bath finish the second level.

First floor — 911 sq. ft.
Second floor — 576 sq. ft.

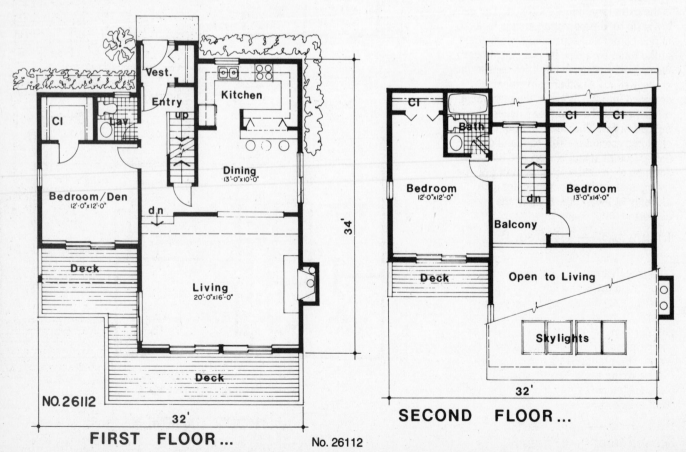

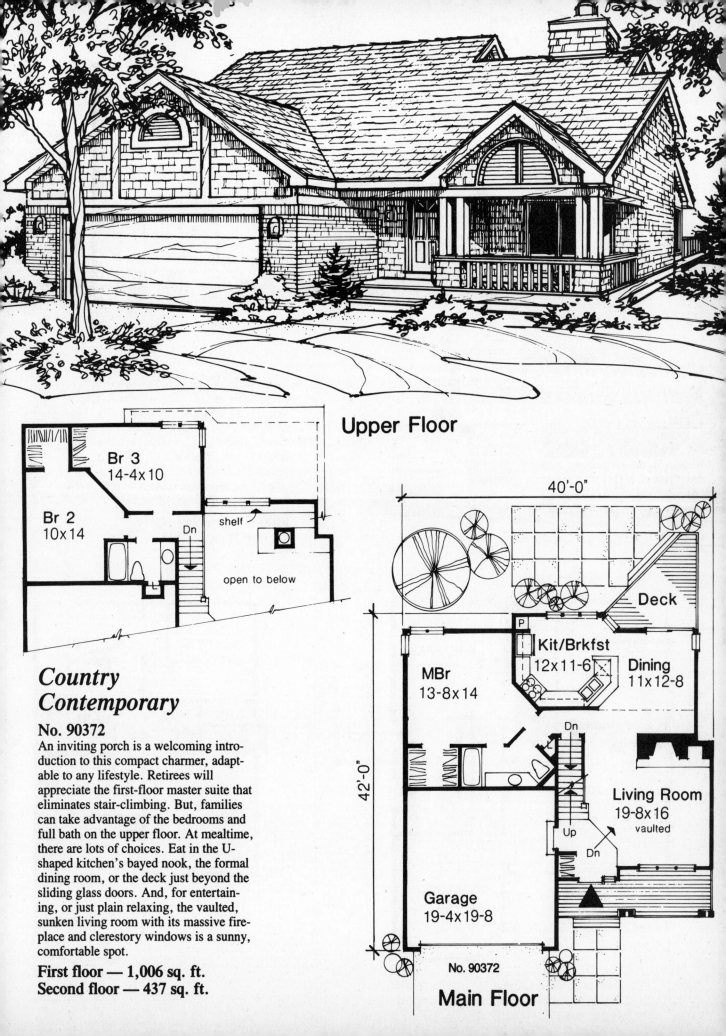

Upper Floor

Br 3
14-4 x 10

Br 2
10 x 14

shelf

Dn

open to below

Country Contemporary

No. 90372

An inviting porch is a welcoming intro-duction to this compact charmer, adapt-able to any lifestyle. Retirees will appreciate the first-floor master suite that eliminates stair-climbing. But, families can take advantage of the bedrooms and full bath on the upper floor. At mealtime, there are lots of choices. Eat in the U-shaped kitchen's bayed nook, the formal dining room, or the deck just beyond the sliding glass doors. And, for entertain-ing, or just plain relaxing, the vaulted, sunken living room with its massive fire-place and clerestory windows is a sunny, comfortable spot.

First floor — 1,006 sq. ft.
Second floor — 437 sq. ft.

40'-0"

Deck

Kit/Brkfst
12 x 11-6

Dining
11 x 12-8

MBr
13-8 x 14

Dn

42'-0"

P

Up

Dn

Living Room
19-8 x 16
vaulted

Garage
19-4 x 19-8

No. 90372

Main Floor

Compact Victorian Ideal For Narrow Lot

ELEVATION A

No. 90406

This compact Victorian design incorporates four bedrooms and three full baths into a thirty foot wide home. The upstairs master suite features two closets, an oversized tub and a sitting room with vaulted ceiling and bay window. Two additional bedrooms and a second full bath are included in the upper level. A fourth bed-

room and third full bath on the main floor can serve as an in-law or guest suite. Between the dining and breakfast rooms is a galley kitchen. The dining room has a bay window and the breakfast room a utility nook. A large parlor with a raised-hearth fireplace completes the main floor. The porches add to the overall exterior appearance and help to protect the front and side entrances.

First floor — 954 sq. ft.
Second floor — 783 sq. ft.

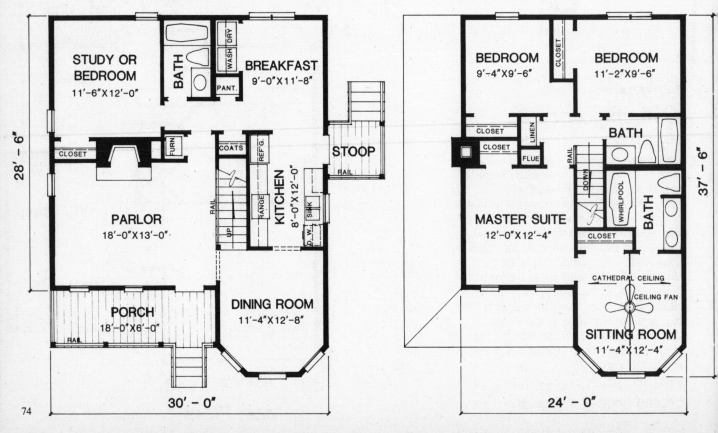

Balcony Enriches Bedrooms

No. 10128

A splendid 23 foot balcony enhances the appeal of the two bedrooms of this split level plan. Stone veneer, ornamental railings, and French doors add to the eye catching exterior. Effective zoning further distinguishes the interior of this home. The foyer channels traffic to the living room, kitchen, or upstairs. A well proportioned kitchen serves the adjacent dining area with ease and the terrace beyond. The lower level has laundry facilities and a double garage.

Living area — 1,344 sq. ft.
Garage level — 720 sq. ft.

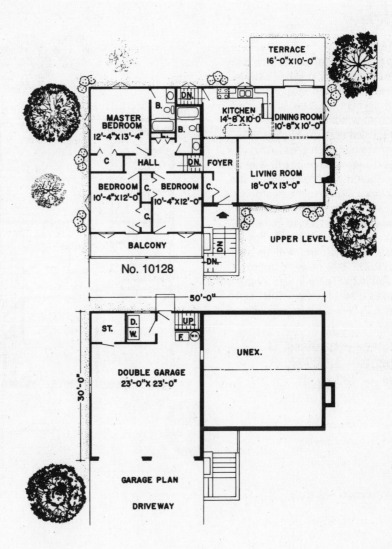

Inexpensive Ranch Design

No. 20062

This attractive, inexpensive ranch home has a brick and vertical siding exterior. The interior has a well set-up kitchen area with its own breakfast area by a large picture window. A formal dining room is located near the kitchen. The living room has one open beam across a sloping ceiling. A large hearth is in front of a woodburning fireplace. Inside the front entrance a tiled foyer incorporates closet space and has many different room entrances through which an individual can walk. The master bedroom has an extremely large bath area with its own walk-in closet. Two other bedrooms share a full bath. There is also a linen closet and a closet for the washer and dryer area. A two-car garage is offered in this plan.

First floor — 1,500 sq. ft.
Basement — 1,500 sq. ft.
Garage — 482 sq. ft.

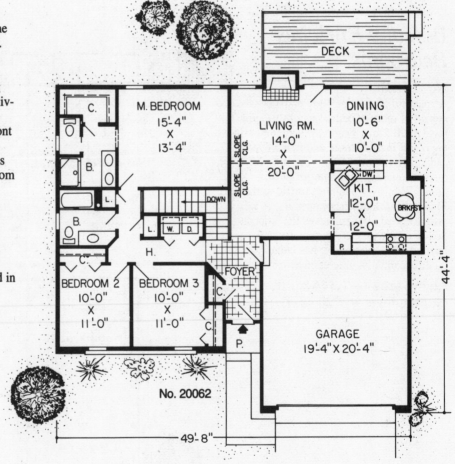

One-Level Living is a Breeze

No. 10656

Zoned for privacy and convenience, this contemporary ranch is a perfect home for people who like to entertain. The central foyer divides quiet and active areas. Sound deadening closets and a full bath with double vanities keep the noise to a minimum in the bedroom wing. The deck off the master suite is a nice, private retreat for sunbathing or stargazing. Look at the recessed ceilings and bay windows in the dining room off the foyer. What a beautiful room for a candlelit dinner. Living areas at the rear of the house surround a brick patio so guests can enjoy the outdoors in nice weather. And, the open plan of the kitchen, nook, and vaulted great room keep traffic flowing smoothly, even when there's a crowd.

First floor — 1,899 sq. ft.
Basement — 1,890 sq. ft.
Garage — 530 sq. ft.

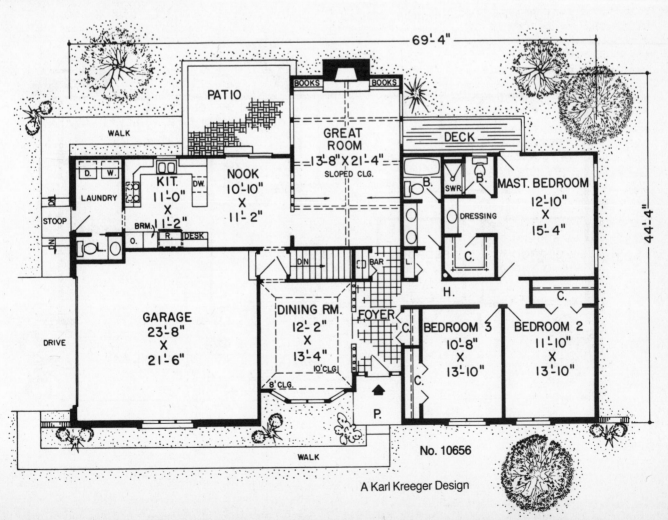

No. 10656

A Karl Kreeger Design

Distinctive Living

No. 8266

You'll enjoy this combination of an attractive exterior and a most convenient and livable interior. There are three large bedrooms and two full baths. The living room shows an interior wall fireplace. The modern built-in kitchen is flanked to the left by the dining room and on the right by a dinette. Note the siding and the folding doors between the kitchen, the dining room and living room. A stairway leads to the basement which provides more utility space as well as future recreational areas.

First floor — 1,604 sq. ft.
Garage — 455 sq. ft.
Basement — 1,604 sq. ft.

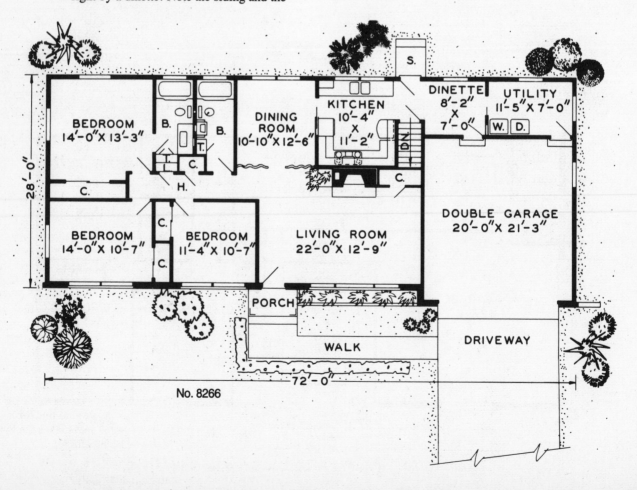

No. 8266

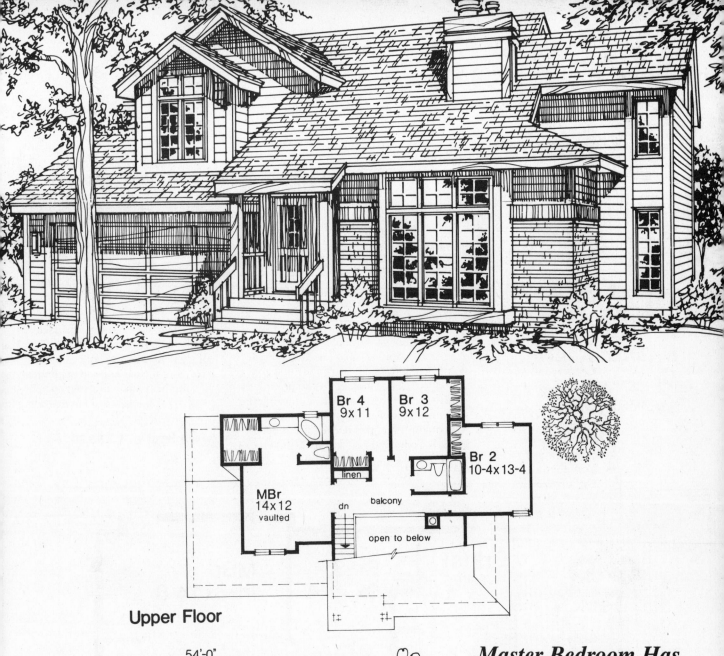

Upper Floor

Br 4
9x11

Br 3
9x12

Br 2
10-4x13-4

linen

MBr
14x12
vaulted

balcony

dn

open to below

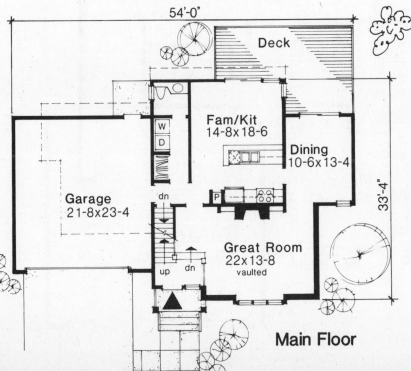

54'-0"

Deck

Fam/Kit
14-8x18-6

Dining
10-6x13-4

W
D

Garage
21-8x23-4

P

dn

up   dn

Great Room
22x13-8
vaulted

33'-4"

Main Floor

Master Bedroom Has a Vaulted Ceiling

No. 90371

Young families and the move up market are looking for lots of liveable space in a good looking package that combines a look of substance with sophistication. This kind of house has that design character with an exterior that uses masonry and rough siding under a sweeping roof line, an interior that lets space flow and accepts high impact views. The entry and great room vault up to the hall balcony above, the country kitchen is great for family doings, the master bedroom suite emphasizes good walk in closet space and a luxurious bathroom. And note how well the house hugs the ground line for a two story home, a look that makes the house one of the 80's generation.

First floor — 952 sq. ft.
Second floor — 915 sq. ft.

Detailed Ranch Design

No. 90360

Stylish houses to suit the higher design expectations of the sophisticated first time and move up buyer need to present lot of visible value. Starting with the very 1980's exterior look of this home with its arcaded living room sash, thru its interior vaulted spaces and interesting master bedroom suite, this house says "buy me". Foundation offsets are kept to the front where they count for character; simple main roof frames over main house body and master bedroom cantilever. Note, too, the easy option of eliminating the third bedroom closet and opening this room to the kitchen as a family room plus two bedroom home.

Main level — 1,283 sq. ft.

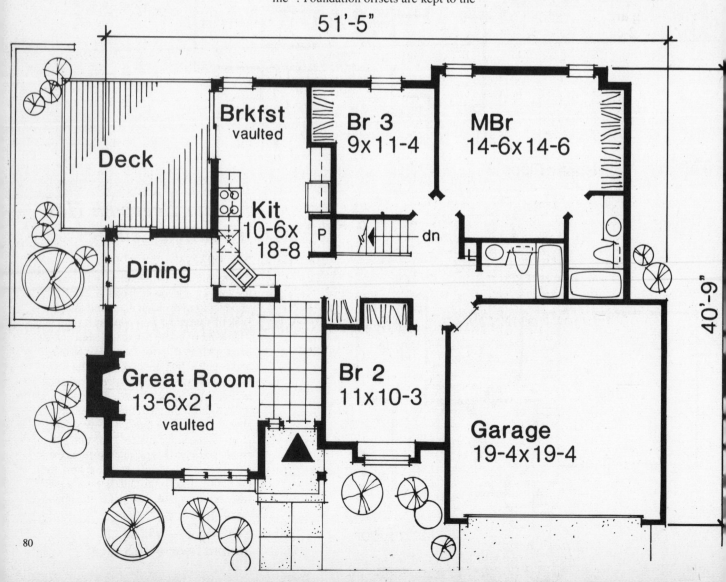

Cathedral Window Graced by Massive Arch

No. 20066

A tiled threshold provides a distinctive entrance into this spacious home. There's room for gracious living everywhere, from the comfortable living room with a wood-burning fireplace and tiled hearth, to the elegant dining room with a vaulted ceiling, to the outside deck. Plan your meals in a kitchen that has all the right ingredients: a central work island, pantry, planning desk, and breakfast area. A decorative ceiling will delight your eye in the master suite, which includes a full bath and bow window.

First floor — 1,850 sq. ft.
Basement — 1,850 sq. ft.
Garage — 503 sq. ft.

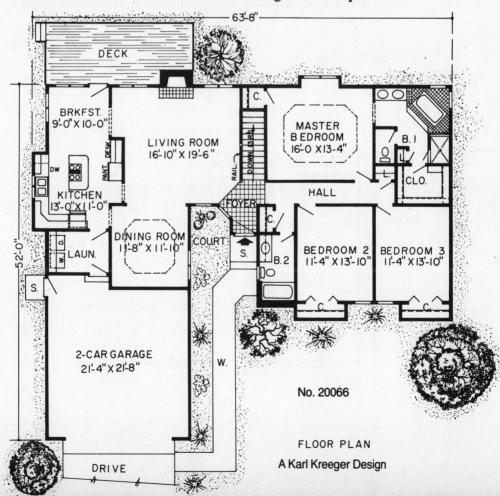

No. 20066

FLOOR PLAN

A Karl Kreeger Design

Fireplace Dominates Rustic Design

No. 90409

The ample porch of this charming home deserves a rocking chair, and there's room for two or three if you'd like. The front entry opens to an expansive great room with a soaring cathedral ceiling.

Flanked by the master suite and two bedrooms with a full bath, the great room is separated from formal dining by a massive fireplace. The convenient galley kitchen adjoins a sunny breakfast nook, perfect for informal family dining.

Living area — 1,670 sq. ft.

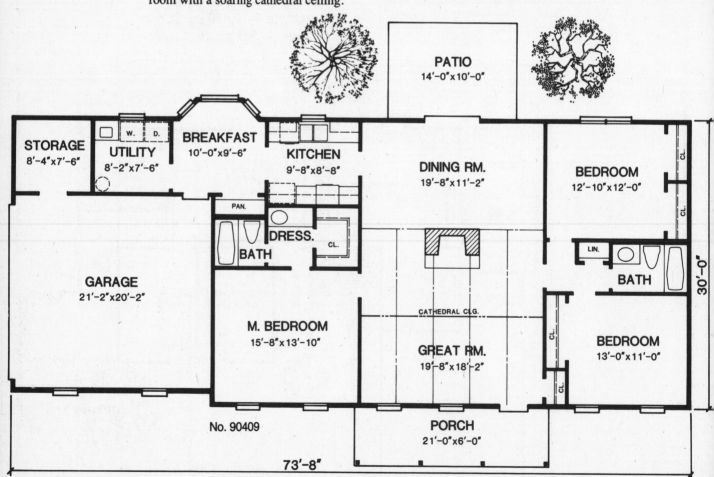

PATIO
14'-0"x10'-0"

STORAGE
8'-4"x7'-6"

W. D.

UTILITY
8'-2"x7'-6"

BREAKFAST
10'-0"x9'-6"

KITCHEN
9'-8"x8'-8"

DINING RM.
19'-8"x11'-2"

BEDROOM
12'-10"x12'-0"

CL.

CL.

PAN.

DRESS.

CL.

BATH

LIN.

GARAGE
21'-2"x20'-2"

BATH

M. BEDROOM
15'-8"x13'-10"

CATHEDRAL CLG.

CL.

GREAT RM.
19'-8"x18'-2"

CL.

BEDROOM
13'-0"x11'-0"

30'-0"

No. 90409

PORCH
21'-0"x6'-0"

73'-8"

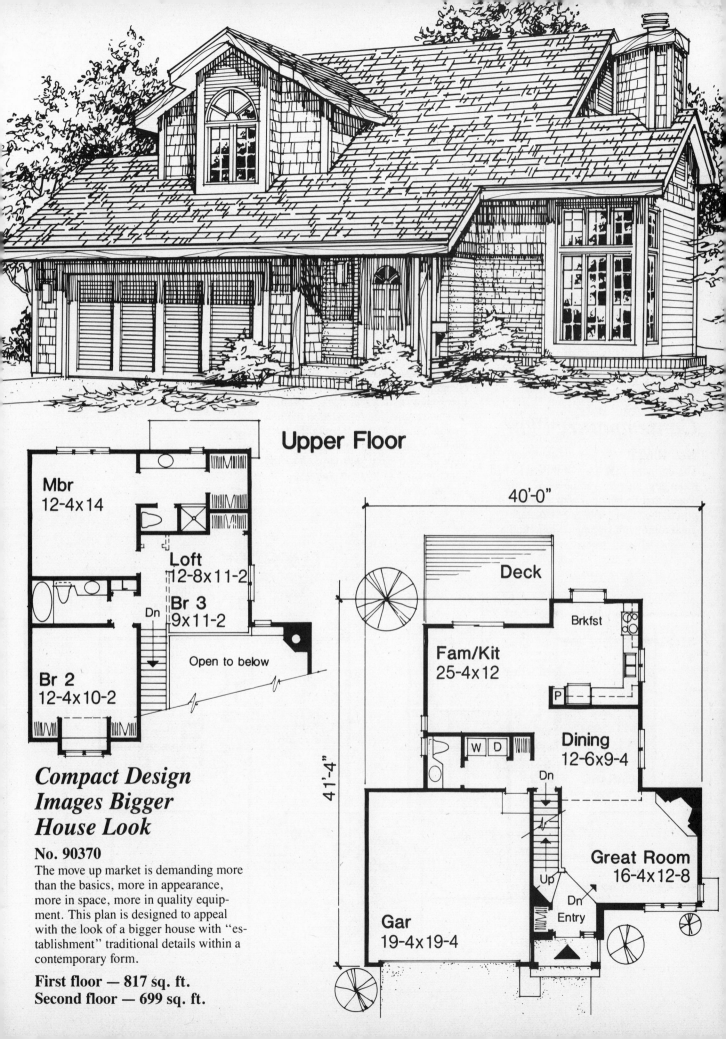

Upper Floor

Mbr
12-4x14

Loft
12-8x11-2

Br 3
9x11-2

Dn

Open to below

Br 2
12-4x10-2

40'-0"

Deck

Brkfst

Fam/Kit
25-4x12

P

41'-4"

W D

Dining
12-6x9-4

Dn

Up

Gar
19-4x19-4

Dn
Entry

Great Room
16-4x12-8

Compact Design Images Bigger House Look

No. 90370
The move up market is demanding more than the basics, more in appearance, more in space, more in quality equipment. This plan is designed to appeal with the look of a bigger house with "establishment" traditional details within a contemporary form.

First floor — 817 sq. ft.
Second floor — 699 sq. ft.

Master Retreat Crowns Contemporary Plan

No. 10625

The dramatic roof lines of this three-bedroom gem only hint at the wonderful angles that lie inside. From a sheltered porch, the foyer leads to a two-story great room with sloping ceilings and a huge fireplace. For outdoor lovers, the open plan unites the kitchen, dining, and living areas with a rear deck. Upstairs, dramatic angles are repeated in the master suite, tucked away from other parts of the house on its own landing. A few steps up, two more bedrooms share the upper reaches of this intriguing contemporary.

First floor — 990 sq. ft.
Second floor — 980 sq. ft.
Garage — 450 sq. ft.

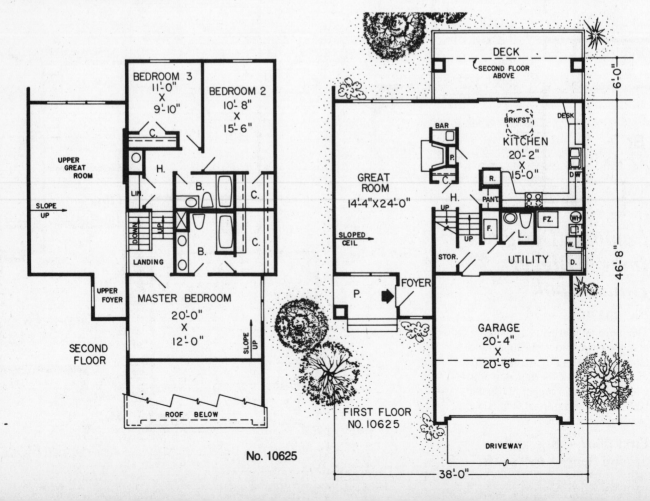

No. 10625

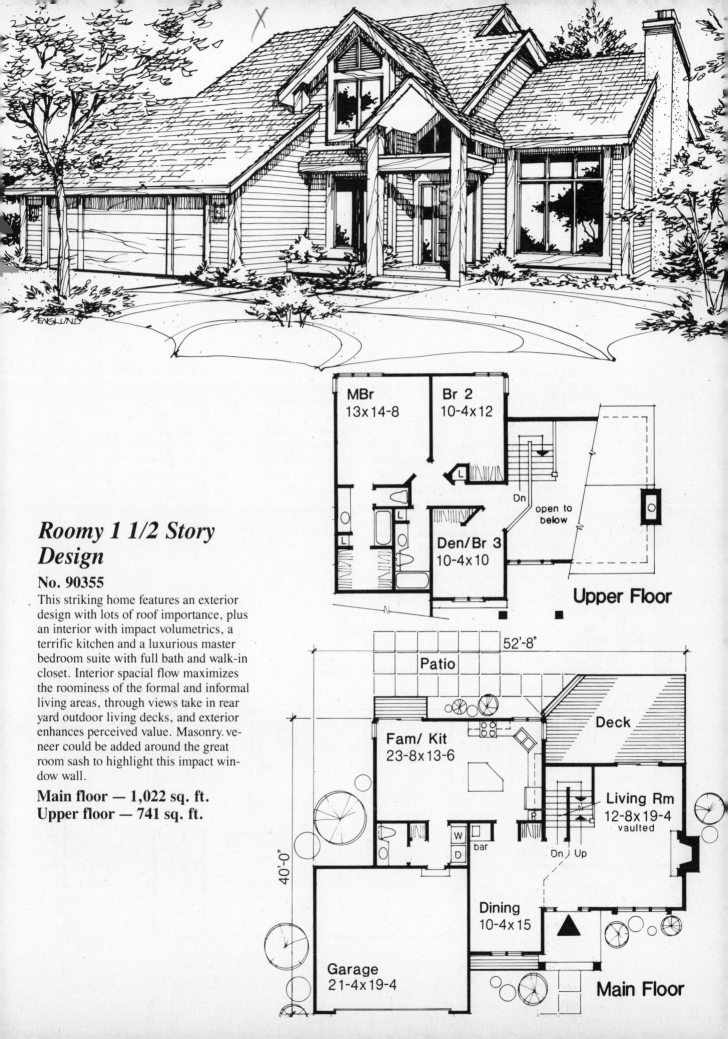

Roomy 1 1/2 Story Design

No. 90355

This striking home features an exterior design with lots of roof importance, plus an interior with impact volumetrics, a terrific kitchen and a luxurious master bedroom suite with full bath and walk-in closet. Interior spacial flow maximizes the roominess of the formal and informal living areas, through views take in rear yard outdoor living decks, and exterior enhances perceived value. Masonry veneer could be added around the great room sash to highlight this impact window wall.

Main floor — 1,022 sq. ft.
Upper floor — 741 sq. ft.

MBr
13x14-8

Br 2
10-4x12

Den/Br 3
10-4x10

Dn

open to below

L

Upper Floor

52'-8"

Patio

Deck

Fam/ Kit
23-8x13-6

W D   bar

Living Rm
12-8x19-4
vaulted

Dn   Up

P

Dining
10-4x15

40'-0"

Garage
21-4x19-4

Main Floor

Your Classic Hideaway

No. 90423

Don't limit this design. Such a tranquil plan could maximize a vacation or suit retirement, as well as be a wonderful family home. It's large enough to welcome a crowd, but small enough for easy upkeep. The only stairs go to the basement. The lavish master suite, with its sunken tub, melts away cares. Either guest bedroom is big enough for two. The lovely fireplace is both cozy and a source of heat for the core area of the home. Note how the country kitchen connects to the large dining and living space. With a screened porch, laundry alcove, and large garage for storage, you'll have everything you need with a minimum of maintenance and cleaning. Specify basement, crawlspace, or slab foundation.

Living area — 1,773 sq. ft.
Screened porch — 240 sq. ft.

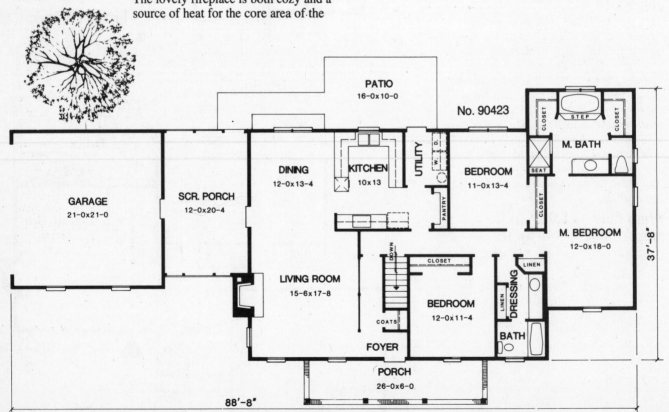

A One Story Home with a New Angle

No. 10600

The large fieldstone fireplace in the living room mirrors the rustic facade of this 3 bedroom home. And, interesting ceiling angles occur in every room. Protected from street noise by a 2 car garage, the two front bedrooms are flooded with light from double windows. Across the hall, the master bedroom suite boasts a huge walk-in closet, a bump out window area with access to the patio, and a full bath with dual sinks. Another full bath and laundry room are steps away. The common living area, with a bay windowed breakfast nook linking kitchen and formal dining room, makes this a convenient design for a busy family.

First floor — 1,219 sq. ft.
Garage — 410 sq. ft.

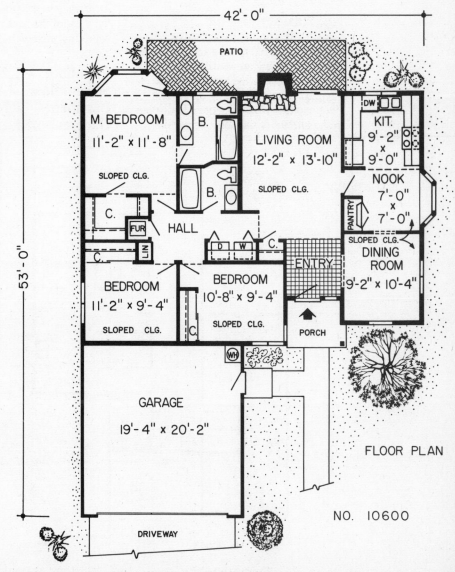

42'-0"

53'-0"

PATIO

M. BEDROOM
11'-2" x 11'-8"

SLOPED CLG.

B.

LIVING ROOM
12'-2" x 13'-10"

SLOPED CLG.

DW

KIT.
9'-2" x 9'-0"

NOOK
7'-0" x 7'-0"

C.

FUR

LIN

HALL

B.

PANTRY

SLOPED CLG.

DINING ROOM
9'-2" x 10'-4"

C.

D W

C.

ENTRY

BEDROOM
11'-2" x 9'-4"

SLOPED CLG.

C.

BEDROOM
10'-8" x 9'-4"

SLOPED CLG.

PORCH

WH

GARAGE
19'-4" x 20'-2"

FLOOR PLAN

NO. 10600

DRIVEWAY

Wonderful Views Everywhere

No. 20068

Consider this home if your backyard is something special in each season. Both living and dining areas offer broad views across the deck to the beautiful scene beyond. Even the balcony on the 2nd floor captures it all. The open floor plan in the interior of the home brings the view to the kitchen and front hall as well. The master bedroom, with a fabulous walk-in closet and lavish bath, maintains its privacy to the side while indulging in the view of the backyard. The 2nd floor bedrooms are notable for the huge closets.

First floor — 1,266 sq. ft.
Second floor — 489 sq. ft.
Basement — 1,266 sq. ft.
Garage — 484 sq. ft.

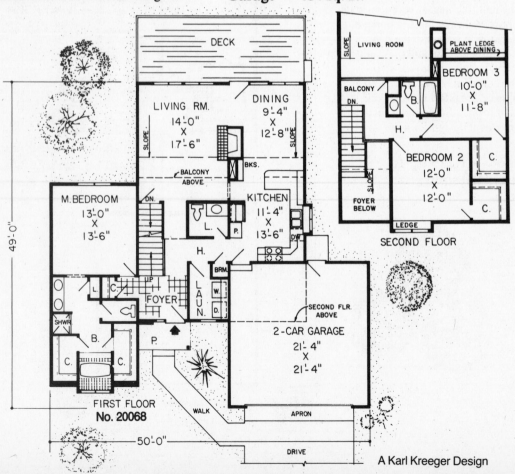

A Karl Kreeger Design

Bridge Adds Interior Drama

No. 20059

An upstairs bridge overlooks the foyer and living room in this dynamic design. Both the living and dining rooms have access to the rear deck. The kitchen has an adjoining breakfast area and a large pantry. The master bedroom has a spacious bath and walk-in closet. The other two bedrooms and bath are located on the second floor.

First floor — 1,234 sq. ft.
Second floor — 520 sq. ft.
Basement — 1,234 sq. ft.
Garage — 477 sq. ft.

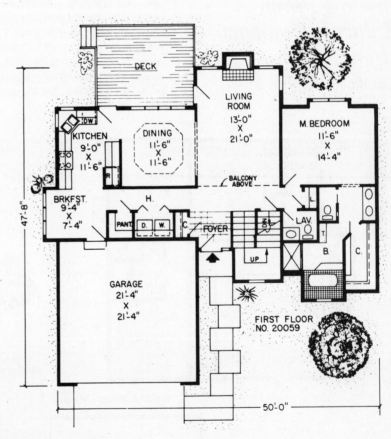

A Karl Kreeger Design

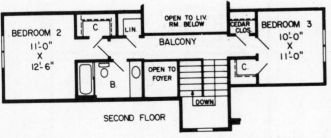

Inviting Porch Enlarges Compact Home

No. 10646

This modified cape with attached two car garage can house a growing family for a bargain price. Double doors in the cozy living room open to the bay-windowed family room with fireplace and patio access. Eat in the family-size kitchen or formal dining room. Up the central stairway, the vaulted ceiling in the master suite creates a spacious feeling. Three other bedrooms and a bath share the second floor.

First floor — 930 sq. ft.
Second floor — 980 sq. ft
Basement — 900 sq. ft.
Garage — 484 sq. ft.

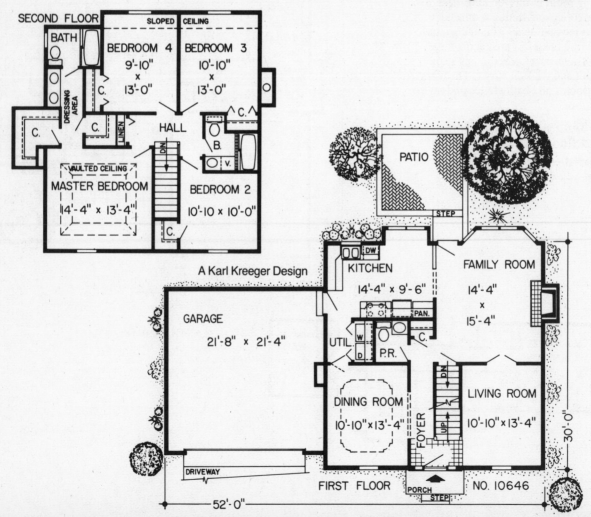

A Karl Kreeger Design

Elegant Design Offers Special Living

No. 10521

This well-crafted design features four
bedrooms, three baths and a balcony
overlooking the two-story foyer. The
master suite includes a five-piece bath,
an oversized walk-in closet and a separate linen closet. The kitchen has a
breakfast nook and includes both a desk
and pantry. The formal living room with
fireplace has direct access to the rear
deck.

First floor — 1,191 sq. ft.
Second floor — 699 sq. ft.
Basement — 1,191 sq.ft.
Garage — 454 sq. ft.

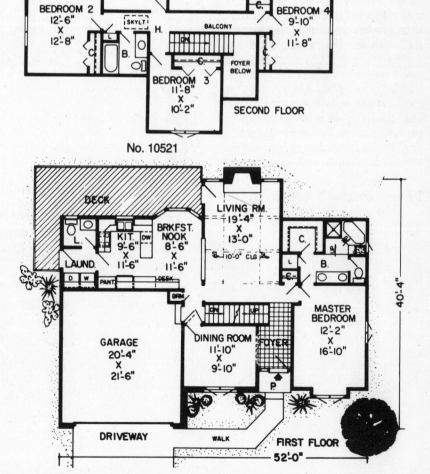

No. 10521

A Karl Kreeger Design

Open Floor Plan Enhanced by Sloped Ceilings

No. 90125

A step down from the tiled entrance area, guests may overlook an expansive living area composed of the great room and the dining room. Warmed by a fireplace and further enhanced by sliding doors opening onto the patio, this welcoming area is easily served by the L-shaped kitchen which shares a snack bar with the dining room. The three bedrooms are separated from the living areas by the careful placement of the bathrooms and the laundry. The master bedroom features two closets, including a walk-in, plus a private bath.

Living area — 1,440 sq. ft.

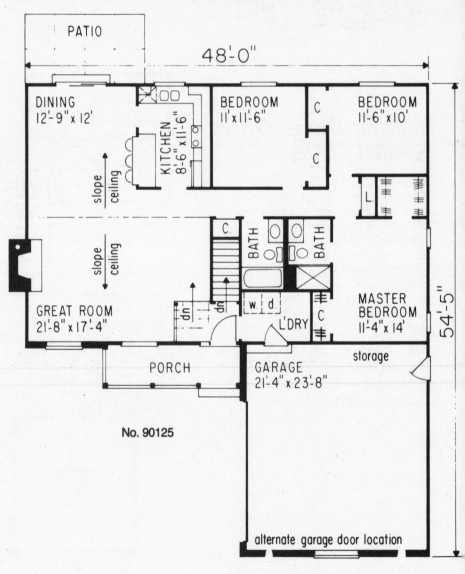

48'-0"

PATIO

DINING
12'-9" x 12'

KITCHEN
8'-6" x 11'-6"

BEDROOM
11' x 11'-6"

C

BEDROOM
11'-6" x 10'

C

slope ceiling

slope ceiling

C.

L.

BATH

BATH

GREAT ROOM
21'-8" x 17'-4"

w d

dn dn

L'DRY

C

MASTER BEDROOM
11'-4" x 14'

54'-5"

storage

PORCH

GARAGE
21'-4" x 23'-8"

No. 90125

alternate garage door location

A-frame Can Be Built Quickly

No. 7664

Easy to apply, red cedar shake shingles are specified for the roof of this A-frame cabin and help make building-it-yourself a feasible and rewarding project. Constructed on a concrete slab, the cabin exudes relaxed informality through the warm natural tones of exposed beams and unfinished wood interior.

Main floor — 560 sq. ft.
Upper level — 240 sq. ft.

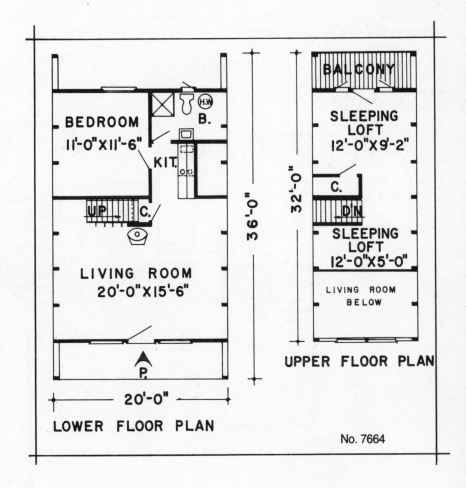

Circular Kitchen Is Center of Family Activities

No. 10514

The unusual design of this kitchen provides the centerpiece for this thoroughly delightful floor plan. The kitchen is further enhanced by the tiled hallways which surround it and delineate the adjacent living areas. The dining room, which opens onto the patio with large glass doors, includes both a built-in hutch and a display case. The large family room has a fireplace with its own wood storage and provides direct access to the sunspace. The master bedroom suite has a private patio, a bay window, five-piece bath, separate vanity and large, walk-in closet.

First floor — 1,954 sq. ft.
Garage — 448 sq. ft.
Sunroom — 144 sq. ft.

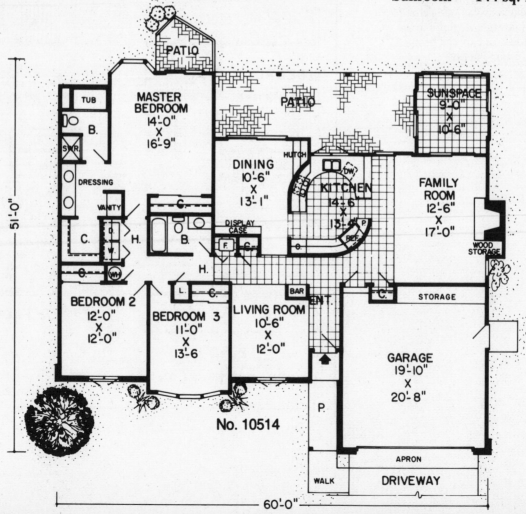

No. 10514

Tradition with a Twist

No. 90933

A traditional exterior hides a multitude of special features that distinguishes this attractive four-bedroom abode. The inviting porch leads into the central foyer, illuminated by a skylight far overhead. You'll find the living and formal dining rooms adjacent to the entry, with informal family areas grouped conveniently at the rear of the house. Separated from the breakfast nook only by a railing, the sunken family room is warmed by a fireplace. Upstairs, the master suite boasts an added attraction — a hidden sundeck, tucked behind the garage for privacy.

First floor — 1,104 sq. ft.
Second floor — 845 sq. ft.

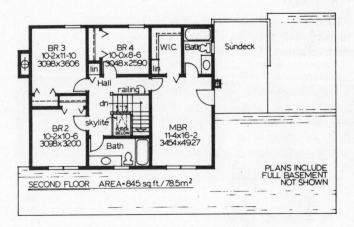

SECOND FLOOR   AREA = 845 sq. ft./78.5m²

No. 90933

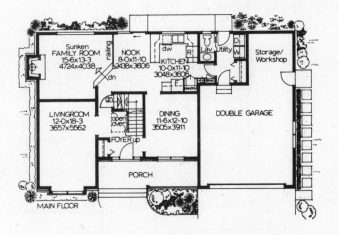

MAIN FLOOR

Railings Unify Open Design

No. 90900

Vaulted ceilings and open spaces highlight the interior of this delightful contemporary design, finished in horizontal cedar with a shake roof. From the moment you step into the foyer with its 2-story ceiling and skylight, you'll be impressed with the spaciousness of this plan. Every room on the main floor is zoned according to function in a step-saving arrangement. A versatile loft upstairs overlooks the living room and foyer below and provides access to three bedrooms and two baths.

Main floor — 1,156 sq. ft.
Second floor — 808 sq. ft.
Unfinished basement — 1,160 sq. ft.

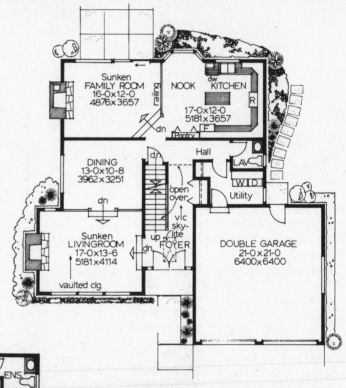

Garage — 473 sq. ft.
Width — 48 ft.
Depth — 47 ft. 6 in.

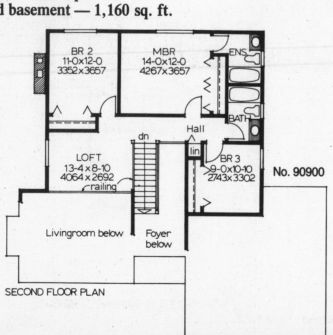

No. 90900

SECOND FLOOR PLAN

Two-Story Solarium Warms Lavish Master Suite

No. 90602

Sophistication abounds in this passive solar split-level. The excellent layout begins with the front-to-back central foyer. To the right are the living and dining areas, featuring a heat-circulating fireplace and a stunning bayed window wall. Large glass doors lead to the south terrace, allowing direct gain heat. Down a half-flight, the recreation room is separated from the solarium by a glass wall. Three bedrooms and two full baths share the upper level.

Upper level — 1,505 sq. ft.
Lower level — 478 sq. ft.
(optional slab construction available)

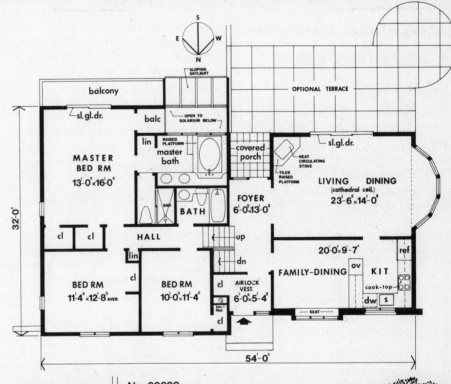

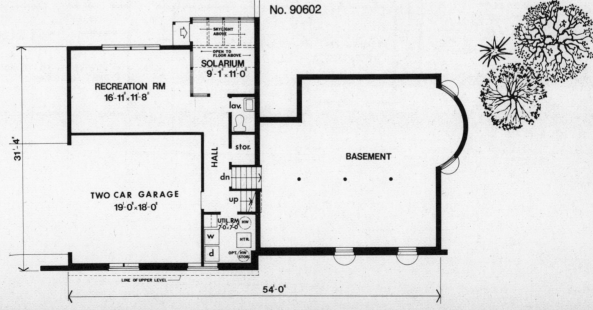

Varied Roof Heights Create Interesting Lines

No. 90601

This rambling one-story Colonial farmhouse packs a lot of living space into its compact plan. The covered porch, enriched by arches, columns and Colonial details, is the focal point of the facade. Inside, the house is zoned for convenience. Formal living and dining rooms occupy the front of the house. To the rear are the family room, island kitchen, and dinette. The family room features a heat-circulating fireplace, visible from the entrance foyer, and sliding glass doors to the large rear patio. Three bedrooms and two baths are away from the action in a private wing.

Total living area — 1,536 sq. ft. (Optional slab construction available)

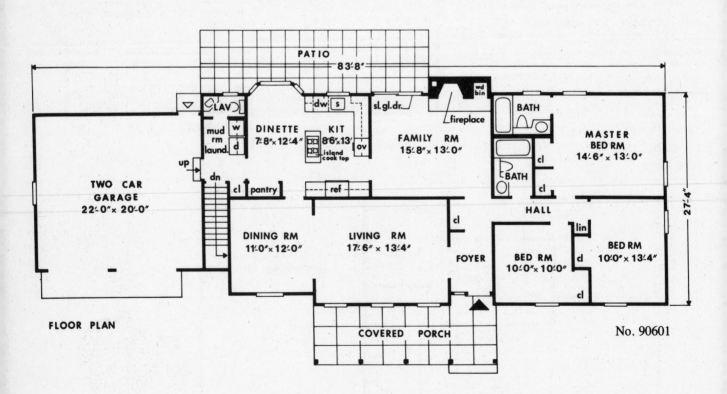

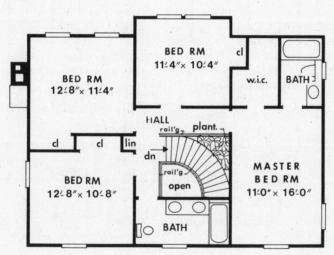

BED RM
12'8" × 11'4"

BED RM
11'4" × 10'4"

cl

w.i.c.

BATH

cl   cl   lin

BED RM
12'8" × 10'8"

HALL

rail'g

plant.

dn

rail'g
open

MASTER
BED RM
11'0" × 16'0"

BATH

No. 90606

Traditional Elements Combine in Friendly Colonial

No. 90606

Casual living is the theme of this elegant Farmhouse Colonial. A beautiful circular stair ascends from the central foyer, flanked by the formal living and dining rooms. The informal family room, accessible from the foyer, captures the Early American style with exposed beams, wood paneling, and brick fireplace wall. A separate dinette opens to an efficient kitchen.

First floor — 1,023 sq. ft.
Second floor — 923 sq. ft.
(optional slab construction available)

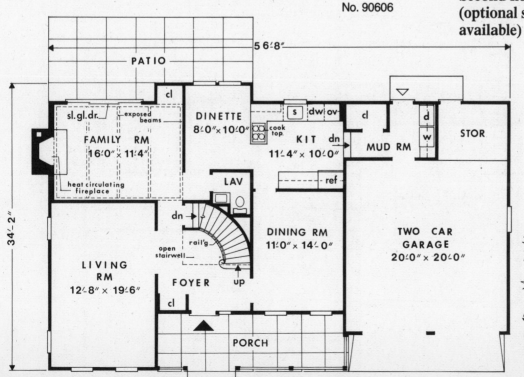

56'8"

PATIO

cl

sl. gl. dr.   exposed beams

FAMILY RM
16'0" × 11'4"

heat circulating fireplace

DINETTE
8'0" × 10'0"

cook top.

s   dw   ov

cl

KIT
11'4" × 10'0"

dn

MUD RM

d
w

STOR

LAV

ref

34'-2"

dn

rail'g

open stairwell

DINING RM
11'0" × 14'0"

TWO CAR
GARAGE
20'0" × 20'0"

LIVING RM
12'8" × 19'6"

FOYER

up

cl

PORCH

Great Traffic Pattern Highlights Home

No. 90901

Victorian styling and economical construction techniques make this a doubly charming design. This is a compact charmer brimming with features: a sheltered entry leading to the two-story foyer; an island kitchen with convenient pass-through to the formal dining room; a cozy living room brightened by a bay window; an airy central hall upstairs surrounded by large bedrooms with plenty of closet space. And look at that lovely master suite with its sitting area in a bay window.

Main floor — 940 sq. ft.
Second floor — 823 sq. ft.
Basement — 940 sq. ft.
Garage — 440 sq. ft.
Width — 54 ft.
Depth — 33 ft.

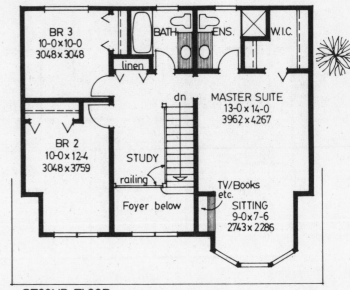

SECOND FLOOR   No. 90901

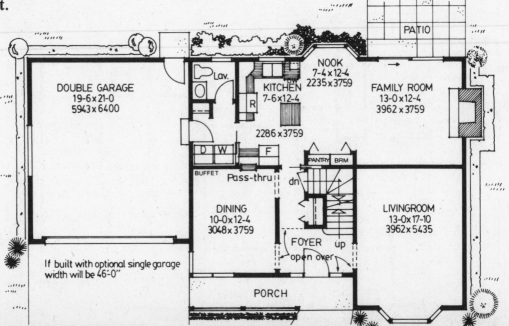

Zoned for Comfort

No. 90610

This ground-hugging ranch was designed for maximum use of three basic living areas. The informal area — fireplaced family room, kitchen, and breakfast room — adjoins a covered porch. The fully-equipped kitchen is easily accessible to the formal dining room, which flows into the living room for convenient entertaining. Well-situated closets and bathrooms set the bedrooms apart from more active areas. The spacious master suite includes plenty of closet space and its own bath. The other bedrooms are served by the lavish hall bath equipped with two basins.

Basic house — 1,771 sq. ft.

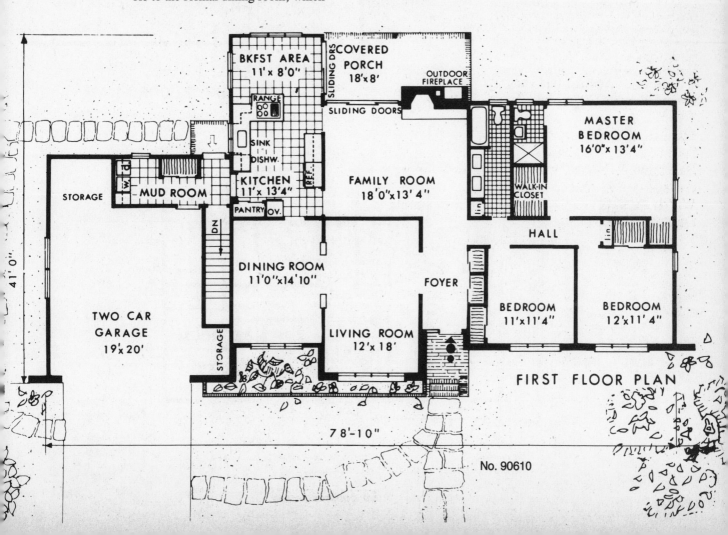

BKFST AREA
11' x 8'0"

COVERED PORCH
18' x 8'

OUTDOOR FIREPLACE

SLIDING DRS

SLIDING DOORS

RANGE

SINK

DISHW.

KITCHEN
11' x 13'4"

PANTRY OV.

REF.

FAMILY ROOM
18'0"x13'4"

MASTER BEDROOM
16'0"x13'4"

WALK-IN CLOSET

HALL

STORAGE

MUD ROOM

W D

DN

DINING ROOM
11'0"x14'10"

FOYER

BEDROOM
11'x11'4"

BEDROOM
12'x11'4"

TWO CAR GARAGE
19'x20'

STORAGE

LIVING ROOM
12'x18'

FIRST FLOOR PLAN

41'0"

78'-10"

No. 90610

Compact Design, Ample Space

No. 10518

Even with less than 1200 square feet, there's plenty of space in this three bedroom, two bath design. A combined living/dining room opens onto the deck which extends the full width of the house. The front kitchen is easily accessible from the entry and is noted for its efficiency. Tucked into the peak of the roof is cozy the master bedroom with its own private bath.

First floor — 864 sq. ft.
Second floor — 307 sq. ft.

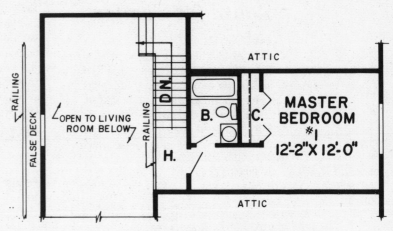

SECOND FLOOR PLAN

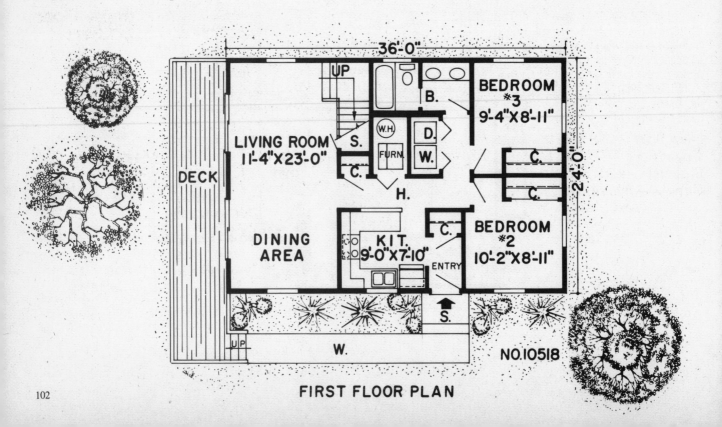

FIRST FLOOR PLAN

Luxurious Master Suite

No. 90329

On the second floor, the roomy master bedroom with its luxurious master bath and dressing area will be a constant delight. Just a step down from the bedroom itself, the bath incorporates an oversized corner tub, a shower, a walk-in closet, and a skylight. The third bedroom could serve as a loft or sitting room. The open staircase spirals down to the first floor great room with its vaulted ceiling, fireplace, and corner of windows. The adjacent dining room has a wet bar and direct access to the large, eat-in kitchen. Additional living space is provided by the family room which opens onto the deck through sliding glass doors.

Main floor — 904 sq. ft.
Upper floor — 797 sq. ft.
Basement — 904 sq. ft.
Garage — 405 sq. ft.

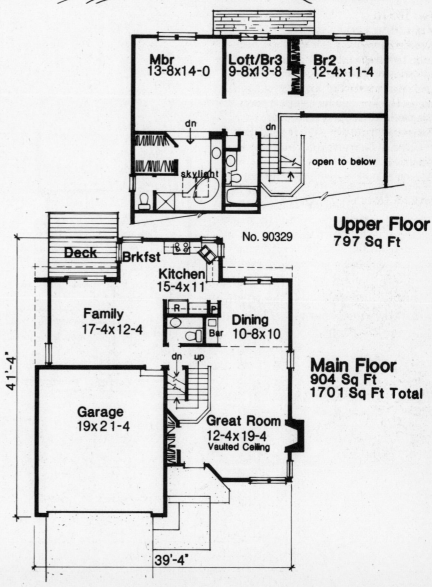

Upper Floor
797 Sq Ft

Mbr 13-8x14-0
Loft/Br3 9-8x13-8
Br2 12-4x11-4
dn
dn
open to below
skylight

No. 90329

Deck
Brkfst
Kitchen 15-4x11
Family 17-4x12-4
R
P
Bar
Dining 10-8x10
dn up
Garage 19x21-4
Great Room 12-4x19-4 Vaulted Ceiling

41'-4"
39'-4"

Main Floor
904 Sq Ft
1701 Sq Ft Total

Arch Recalls Another Era

No. 90675

Massive roof lines pierced with clerestory windows only hint at the interior excitement of this contemporary beauty. The vaulted foyer of this elegant home, graced by doric columns that support an elegant arch, lends an air of ancient Greece to the spacious living and dining rooms. To the right, a well-appointed peninsula kitchen features pass-over convenience to the adjoining dinette bay and family room. Open the sliding glass doors to add an outdoor feeling to every room at the rear of the house. The ample master suite features a private terrace and whirlpool bath. A hall bath serves the other bedrooms in the sleeping wing off the entry.

Main living area — 1,558 sq. ft.
Laundry-mud room — 97 sq. ft.
Garage — 2-car

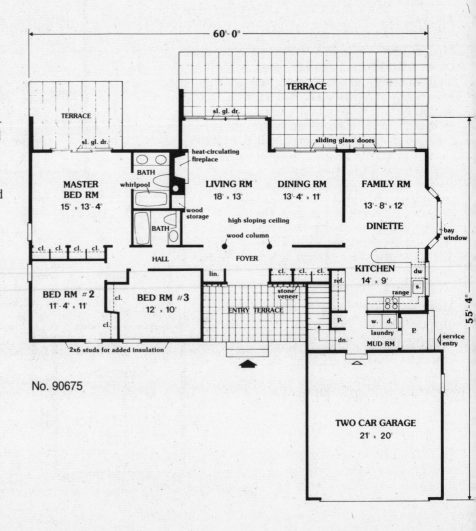

No. 90675

Balcony Overlooks Living Room Below

No. 90356

Smaller houses are getting better all the time, not only in their exterior character and scale, but in their use of spacial volumes and interior finish materials. Here a modest two story gains importance, impact, and perceived value from the sweeping roof lines that make it look larger than it really is. Guests will be impressed by the impact of the vaulted ceiling in the living room up to the balcony hall above, the easy flow of traffic and space in the kitchen and dining areas. Note too, the luxurious master bedroom suite with a window seat bay, walk-in closet, dressing area, and private shower.

Main floor — 674 sq. ft.
Upper floor — 677 sq. ft.

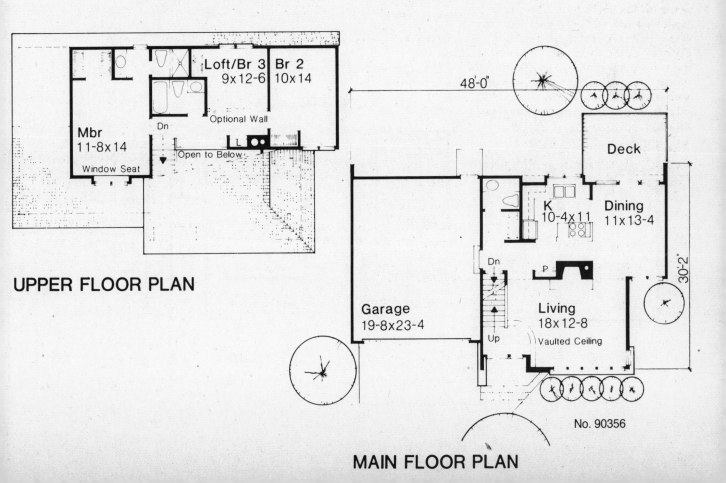

UPPER FLOOR PLAN

Loft/Br 3 9x12-6   Br 2 10x14
Optional Wall
Mbr 11-8x14
Dn
Open to Below
Window Seat

48'-0"
Deck
K 10-4x11   Dining 11x13-4
30'-2"
Dn
P
Garage 19-8x23-4
Living 18x12-8
Up
Vaulted Ceiling

No. 90356

MAIN FLOOR PLAN

Rustic Warmth

No. 90440

While the covered porch and huge, field-stone fireplace lend a rustic air to this three-bedroom classic, the interior is loaded with the amenities you've been seeking. Doesn't a book-lined, fireplaced living room sound nice? Haven't you been longing for a fully-equipped island kitchen? This one adjoins a sunny dining room with sliders to a wood deck. Does the idea of a first-floor master suite just steps away from your morning coffee sound good? Tucked upstairs with another full bath, two bedrooms feature walk-in closets and cozy, sloping ceilings. There's even plenty of extra storage space in the attic.

First floor — 1,100 sq. ft.
Second floor — 664 sq. ft.
Basement — 1,100 sq. ft.

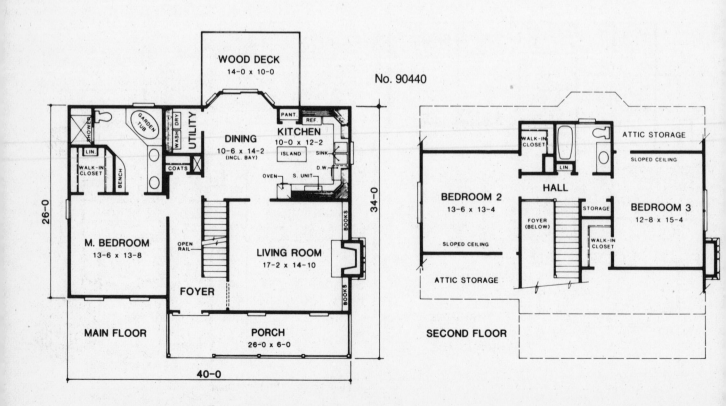

Multi-Level Excitement

No. 20102

With abundant windows, a skylit breakfast room with sliders to a rear deck, and an open plan overlooking the sunken living room below, the foyer level of this distinctive home is a celebration of open space. You'll appreciate the step-saving design of the island kitchen that easily serves both dining rooms. And, you'll enjoy the warmth of the living room fireplace throughout the lower levels of the house. A stairway leads from the foyer to the bedroom level that houses the spacious master suite with a private bath, and two additional bedrooms served by a full bath. The lucky inhabitant of the fourth bedroom, tucked away at the top of the house, will love this private retreat overlooking the two floors below.

First level — 1,003 sq. ft.
Second level — 808 sq. ft.
Third level — 241 sq. ft.
Basement — 573 sq. ft.
Garage — 493 sq. ft.

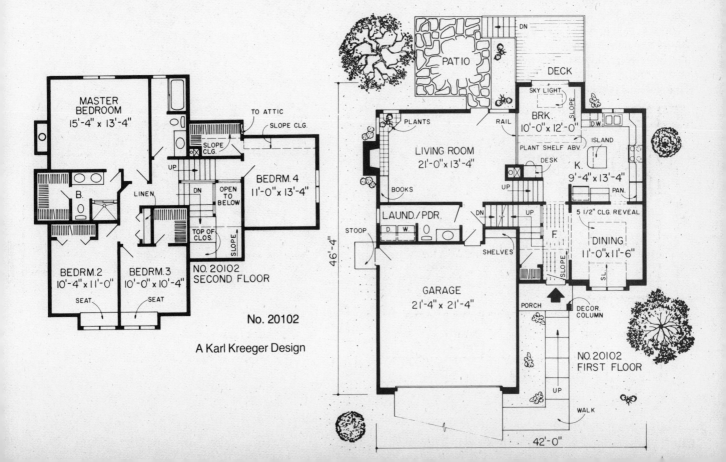

No. 20102

A Karl Kreeger Design

Flexible, Award-winning Design

No. 19938

This two-story home is ideal for those on a budget looking for an adaptable design. The primary living areas on the lower floor complete the basic one-bedroom plan, leaving the upper level, breezeway and garage for completion later, if necessary. The two rooms on the upper level could be used as bedrooms, a hobby room, private office, or almost anything you choose. The family-, dining-, living areas are open to the multi-purpose room above and only partially divided from one another, creating a more spacious and formal atmosphere. You're sure to find that this plan offers a lot for a little.

First floor — 1,090 sq. ft.
Second floor — 580 sq. ft.
Garage — 484 sq. ft.

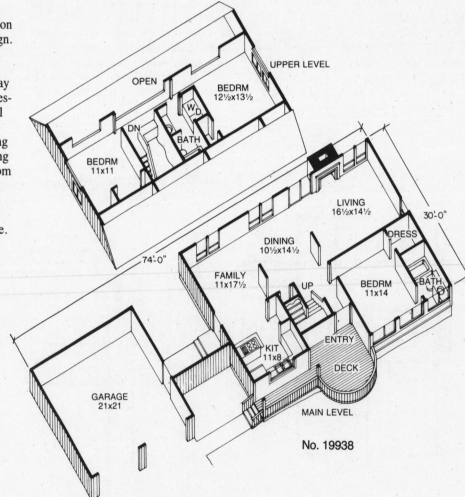

UPPER LEVEL

OPEN

BEDRM
12½x13½

DN

W D

BATH

BEDRM
11x11

LIVING
16½x14½

DRESS

DINING
10½x14½

74'-0"

30'-0"

FAMILY
11x17½

UP

BEDRM
11x14

BATH

KIT
11x8

ENTRY

DECK

GARAGE
21x21

MAIN LEVEL

No. 19938

Soaring Ceilings Add Space and Drama

No. 90288

Here's a one-level home with an airy feeling accentuated by oversized windows and well-placed skylights. You'll love the attractive garden court that adds privacy to the front facing bedroom, the sheltered porch that opens to a central foyer, and the wide-open active areas. Two bedrooms, tucked down a hall off the foyer, include the sunny master suite with its sloping ceilings, private terrace entry, and luxurious garden bath with adjoining dressing room. The gathering room, study, and formal dining room flow together along the rear of the house, sharing the warmth of the gathering room fireplace, and a magnificent view of the terrace. Convenient pass-throughs add to the efficiency of the galley kitchen and adjoining breakfast room.

**Living area — 1,387 sq. ft.
Garage — 2-car**

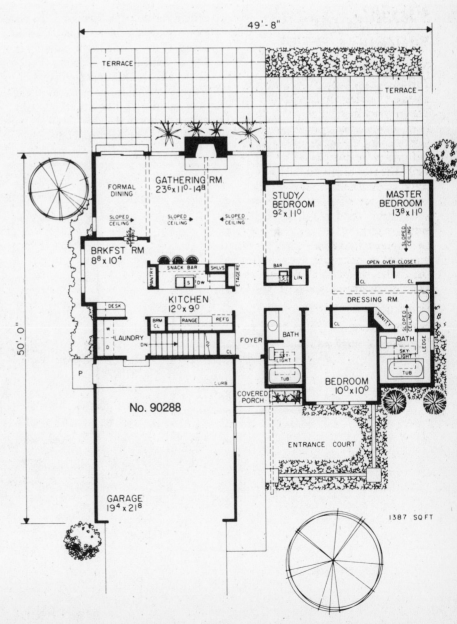

Contemporary Exterior

No. 90327

A spacious feeling is created by the ingenious arrangement of the living areas of this comfortable home. The inviting living room offers a cozy fireplace, a front corner full of windows, a vaulted ceiling and an open staircase. The clerestory windows further accent the open design of the dining room and kitchen. The U-shaped kitchen welcomes cook and tasters alike with its open preparation areas. Secluded from the rest of the main floor and the other two bedrooms, the master bedroom features a walk-in closet and a large, compartmented bath which may also serve as a guest bathroom. Two additional bedrooms and a full bath comprise the upper floor.

Main floor — 846 sq. ft.
Upper floor — 400 sq. ft.
Basement — 846 sq. ft.
Garage — 400 sq. ft.

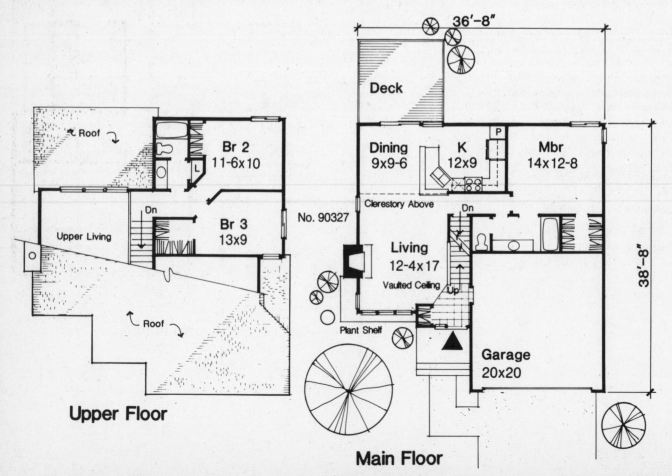

Upper Floor

Main Floor

A-Frame for Year-Round Living

No. 90930

If you have a hillside lot, this open
design may be just what you've been
looking for. With three bedrooms, it's a
perfect plan for your growing family.
The roomy foyer opens to a hallway that
leads to the kitchen, bedrooms, and a
dramatic, vaulted living room with a
massive fireplace. A wrap-around sundeck gives you lots of outdoor living
space. And, upstairs, there's a special
retreat — a luxurious master suite complete with its own private deck.

Main floor — 1,238 sq. ft.
Loft — 464 sq. ft.
Basement — 1,175 sq. ft.
Width — 34 ft.
Depth — 56 ft.

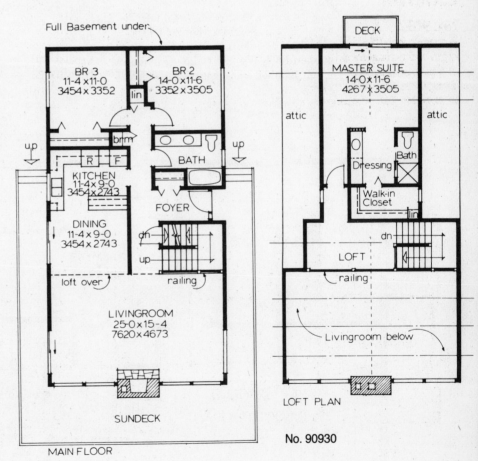

Full Basement under

BR 3
11-4 x 11-0
3454 x 3352

BR 2
14-0 x 11-6
3352 x 3505

lin

up

up

BATH

KITCHEN
11-4 x 9-0
3454 x 2743

R   F

brm

FOYER

DINING
11-4 x 9-0
3454 x 2743

dn

up

loft over

railing

LIVINGROOM
25-0 x 15-4
7620 x 4673

SUNDECK

MAIN FLOOR

DECK

MASTER SUITE
14-0 x 11-6
4267 x 3505

attic

attic

Dressing

Bath

Walk-in
Closet

lin

dn

LOFT

railing

Livingroom below

LOFT PLAN

No. 90930

Comfortable Cottage Suits Narrow Lot

No. 8082

Adaptable to a 50-foot lot, this small cottage boasts an exterior of horizontal siding, brick, and shutters, as well as a cozy interior. Entry is directly into the living room, splashed with light from the plentiful windows. Large enough to entertain a group of people, the living room is shut off from sleeping quarters by a door, which encourages maximum privacy and quiet. Two adequate bedrooms and a full bath are set opposite an extra storage closet.

First floor — 936 sq. ft.
Basement — 936 sq. ft.

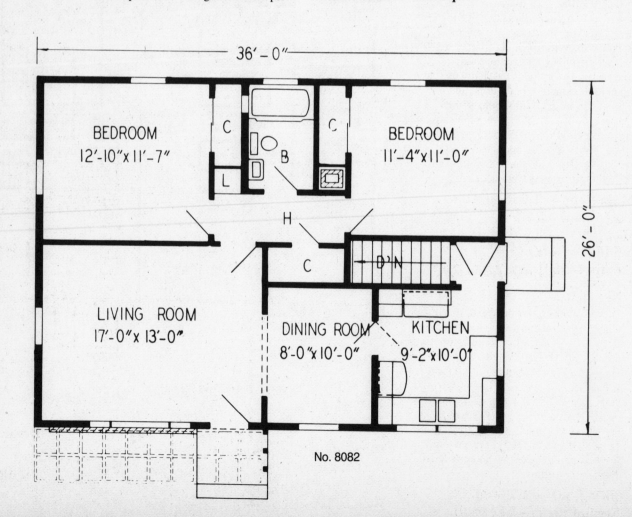

No. 8082

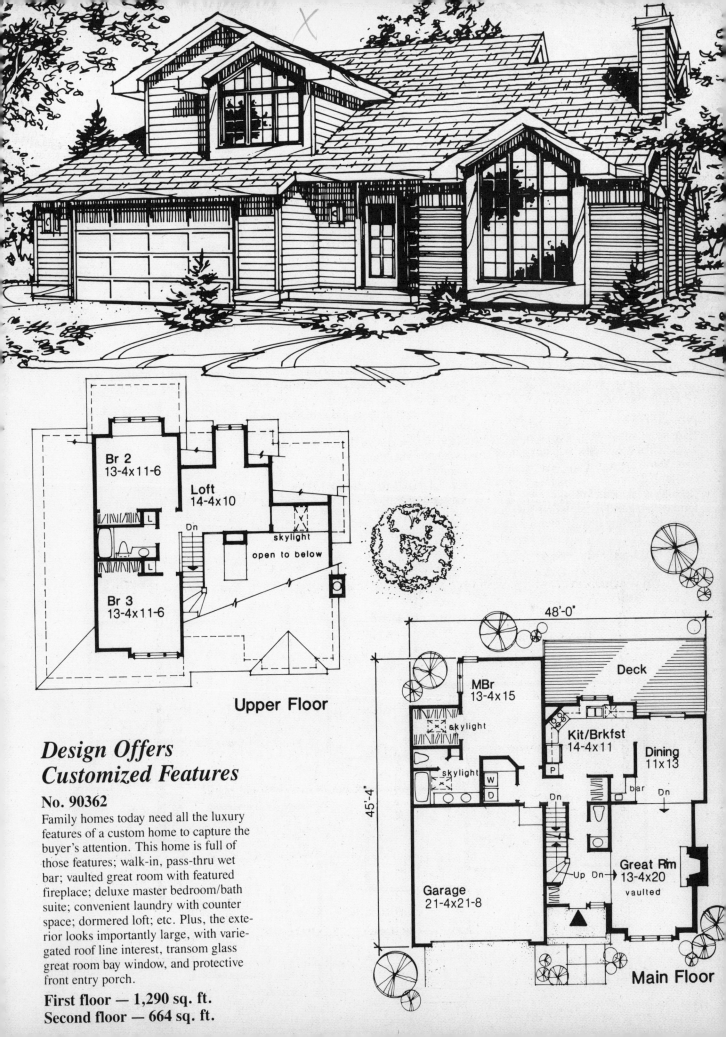

Br 2
13-4x11-6

Loft
14-4x10

Dn

skylight

open to below

Br 3
13-4x11-6

Upper Floor

Design Offers
Customized Features

No. 90362

Family homes today need all the luxury features of a custom home to capture the buyer's attention. This home is full of those features; walk-in, pass-thru wet bar; vaulted great room with featured fireplace; deluxe master bedroom/bath suite; convenient laundry with counter space; dormered loft; etc. Plus, the exterior looks importantly large, with variegated roof line interest, transom glass great room bay window, and protective front entry porch.

First floor — 1,290 sq. ft.
Second floor — 664 sq. ft.

48'-0"

Deck

45'-4"

MBr
13-4x15

skylight

skylight

W
D

Kit/Brkfst
14-4x11

P

Dining
11x13

bar

Dn

Dn

Up Dn

Garage
21-4x21-8

Great Rm
13-4x20
vaulted

Main Floor

Compact and Appealing

No. 20075

Here's an L-shaped country charmer with a porch that demands a rocking chair or two. You'll appreciate the convenient one-level design that separates active and sleeping areas. Right off the foyer, the formal dining and living rooms have a wide-open feeling, thanks to extra wide doorways and a recessed ceiling. The kitchen is centrally located for maximum convenience. For informal family meals, you'll delight in the sunny breakfast nook that links the fireplaced living room and outdoor deck. Enjoy those quiet hours in the three bedrooms separated from family living spaces. With its own double-sink full bath and walk-in closet, the master suite will be your favorite retreat.

First floor — 1,682 sq. ft.
Basement — 1,682 sq. ft.
Garage — 484 sq. ft.

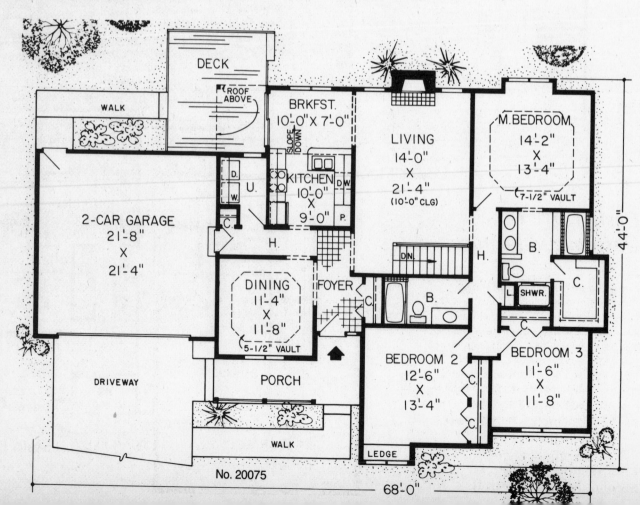

No. 20075

Suited for a Hill

No. 90822

Use this compact A-frame year round or as a vacation retreat. Either way, this practical design is bound to give you pleasure for a long, long time. The main floor, with its vaulted ceilings and field-stone fireplace, combines kitchen, living and dining rooms with two bedrooms and a full bath. The wrap-around sundeck affords lots of outdoor living space. With its soaring views of the floor below, the loft contains the master suite and a perfect place for a home office.

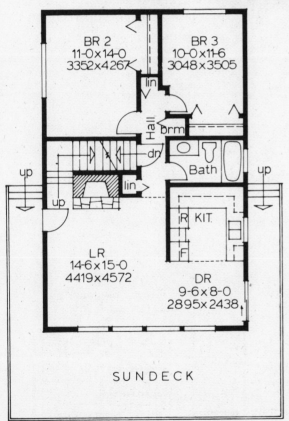

BR 2
11-0×14-0
3352×4267

BR 3
10-0×11-6
3048×3505

lin

Hall

brm

dr

Bath

lin

up

up

up

lin

R KIT.

F

LR
14-6×15-0
4419×4572

DR
9-6×8-0
2895×2438

SUNDECK

MAIN FLOOR   No. 90822

Main floor area — 925 sq. ft.
Loft — 338 sq. ft.
Basement — 864 sq. ft.
Width — 33 ft.
Depth — 47 ft.

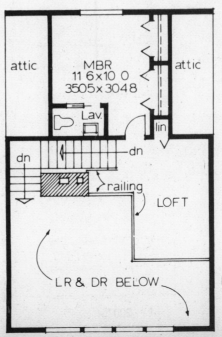

attic

MBR
11 6×10 0
3505×3048

attic

Lav.

lin

dn

dn

railing

LOFT

LR & DR BELOW   LOFT PLAN

Built-In Entertainment Center for Family Fun

No. 90615

Up-to-date features bring this center hall colonial into the 20th century. The focus of the Early American living room is a heat-circulating fireplace, framed by decorative pilasters that support dropped beams. Both dining areas open to the rear terrace through sliding glass doors. And, the convenient mud room provides access to the two car garage. Four bedrooms and two baths, including the spacious master suite, occupy the second floor.

Total living area — 1,973 sq. ft.
Garage — 441 sq. ft.
(optional slab construction available)

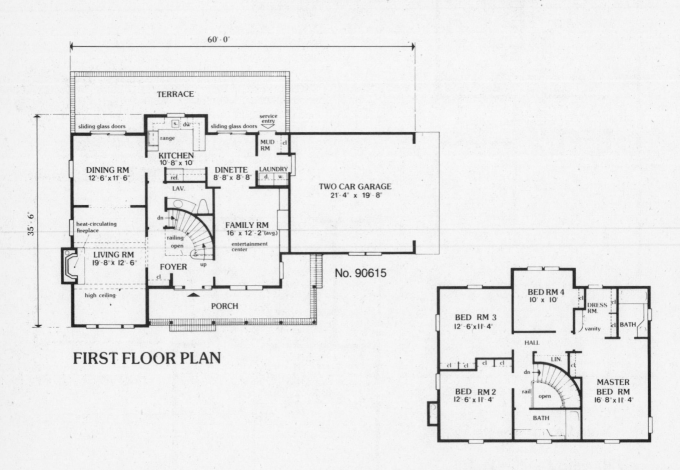

FIRST FLOOR PLAN

SECOND FLOOR PLAN

Intelligent Use of Space

No. 10483

Lots of living is packed into this well designed home which features a combined kitchen and dining room. The highly functional U-shaped kitchen includes a corner sink under double windows. Opening onto the dining room is the living room which is illuminated by both a front picture window and a skylight. Its lovely fireplace makes this an inviting place to gather. The sleeping area of this home contains three bedrooms and two full baths, one of which is a private bath accessed only from the master bedroom.

First floor — 1,025 sq. ft.
Garage — 403 sq. ft.

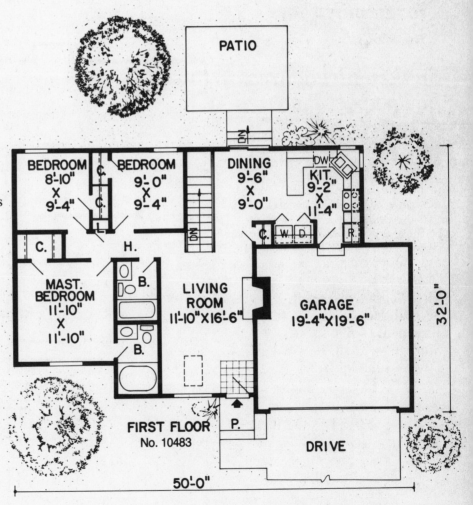

PATIO

BEDROOM
8'-10"
X
9'-4"

C.

BEDROOM
9'-0"
X
9'-4"

DINING
9'-6"
X
9'-0"

DW

KIT
9'-2"
X
11'-4"

C.

C. W D.

R.

H.

MAST.
BEDROOM
11'-10"
X
11'-10"

B.

LIVING
ROOM
11'-10"X16'-6"

GARAGE
19'-4"X19'-6"

B.

P.

FIRST FLOOR
No. 10483

DRIVE

32'-0"

50'-0"

Sunken Living Areas in Compact Plan

No. 26114

Step down from the entry level to the sunken living, dining, and kitchen areas of this floor plan. The fireplaced living room looks out through double sliding glass doors to a wrap-around deck which ends in outside storage. Ceilings slope up above a balcony which also shares the second level with two bedrooms and a bath. An optional third bedroom/den lies on the lower level.

First floor — 696 sq. ft.
Second floor — 416 sq. ft.
Basement — 696 sq. ft.
Storage — 32 sq. ft.
Deck — 232 sq. ft.

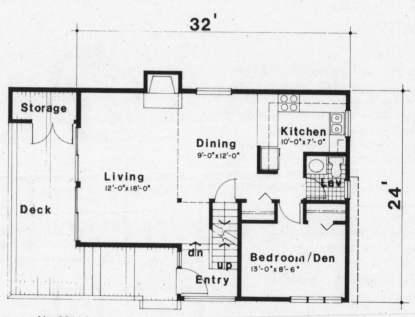

No. 26114

FIRST FLOOR

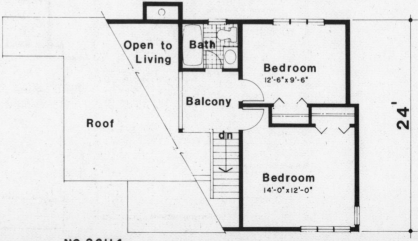

NO. 26114

SECOND FLOOR

First-Time Owner's Delight

No. 20063

A distinctive exterior of wood veneer siding with a large, picture window combines with just a touch of brick to set this simple one and a half story design into a class of its own. On the first level, the foyer leads directly into the living room which has a fireplace and is open to the dining room. The kitchen lies just to the left of the dining room. A laundry room is conveniently placed between the kitchen and the garage. The master bedroom lies on the first floor and has a full bath and walk-in closet. On the second floor two more bedrooms exist and share a full bath. There is also a loft area open to the living room below.

First floor — 1,161 sq. ft.
Second floor — 631 sq. ft.

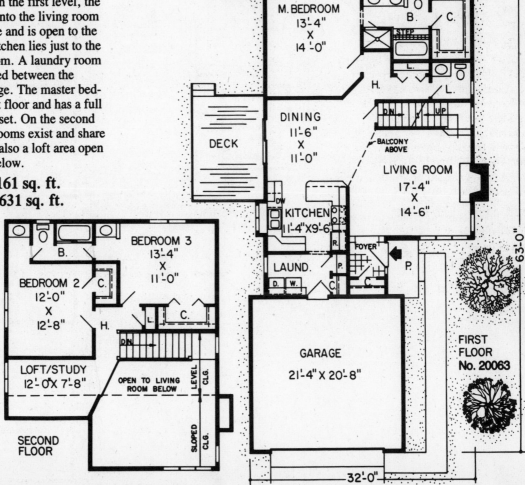

M. BEDROOM
13'-4" X 14'-0"

B.

C.

STEP

H.

L.

DECK

DINING
11'-6" X 11'-0"

DN UP

BALCONY ABOVE

LIVING ROOM
17'-4" X 14'-6"

DW

KITCHEN
11'-4" X 9'-6"

R.

FOYER

LAUND.

P.

P.

D. W.

C.

63'-0"

GARAGE
21'-4" X 20'-8"

FIRST FLOOR
No. 20063

32'-0"

B.

BEDROOM 3
13'-4" X 11'-0"

BEDROOM 2
12'-0" X 12'-8"

C.

H.

L.

C.

DN

LOFT/STUDY
12'-0" X 7'-8"

OPEN TO LIVING ROOM BELOW

LEVEL CLG.

SLOPED CLG.

SECOND FLOOR

Sheltered Porch Graces Family Dwelling

No. 20067

Consider an easy-to-care-for home if you have a growing family. An all wood exterior that relieves you of yearly maintenance is just one of the features. The compact floor plan minimizes housekeeping yet arranges the play area so that an eye can be kept on young children, whether inside or in the backyard. Note touches like the tiled foyer that stops muddy traffic entering from either the front door or garage. Three bedrooms are located near to one another on the same level for nighttime security. The basement provides room for expansion as the children get older.

Living area — 1,459 sq. ft.
Basement — 697 sq. ft.
Garage — 694 sq. ft.

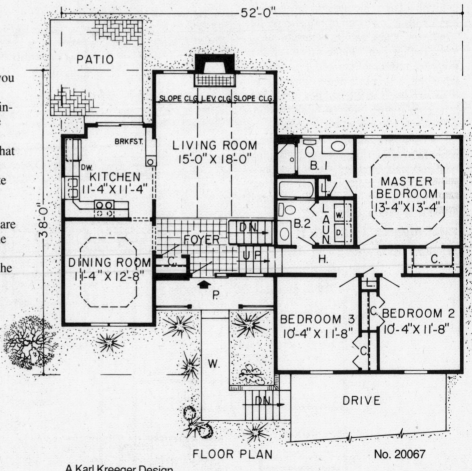

FLOOR PLAN   No. 20067

A Karl Kreeger Design

Feature-packed Living Space

No. 10509

This well-zoned plan incorporates features usually found in much larger houses and does it with style. The living areas extend from the extremely efficient kitchen into the living room and around the corner into the dining area. The living room is accented by sliding doors to the patio and a fireplace with an extended hearth. Separating the living areas from the three bedrooms is the placement of the entry, the laundry and the master bath. The large and inviting master suite has a dressing area, walk-in closet and private patio. The third bedroom has features a built-in dressing table. You'll find that this home receives you well.

First floor — 1,464 sq. ft.
Garage — 528 sq. ft.

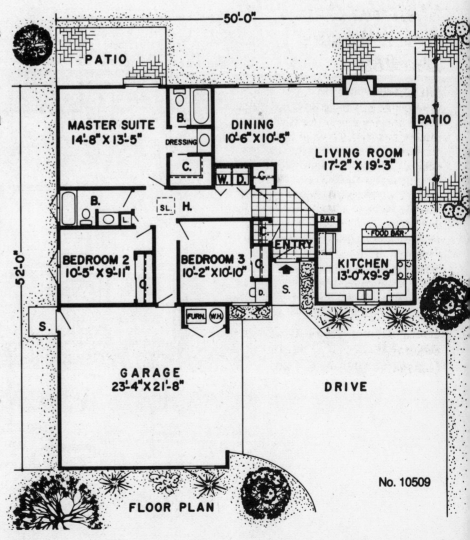

FLOOR PLAN

No. 10509

Storage Space Galore In Garage

No. 20065

This simple design's exterior features a large picture window and rock front. On the first floor from the foyer is a spacious living room with its own wood burning fireplace. The dining room lies in front of the living room and next to the kitchen. From the kitchen to the right is the breakfast room with access to a large outdoor wooden deck. A half bath and laundry facilities are other rooms on the first floor. On the second floor are three bedrooms. Two bedrooms share a full bath with its own skylight, while the master bedroom has its own private bath and walk-in closet. One final feature of this plan is the large amount of storage space available in the two-car garage.

First floor — 936 sq. ft.
Second floor — 777 sq. ft.
Garage/storage — 624 sq. ft.

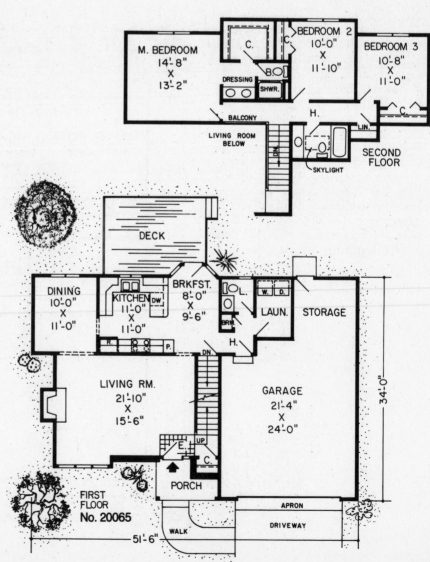

Place This House For Solar Gain

No. 90620

This modest ranch with generous rooms and passive solar features provides comfortable living for the family on a budget. The soaring, skylit central foyer provides access to every room. Straight ahead, the living room, dining room, and greenhouse form a bright, airy arrangement of glass and open space. The adjacent kitchen conveniently opens to a spacious, bay-windowed dinette. A separate wing contains three bedrooms and two baths, including an ample master suite.

Total living area — 1,405 sq. ft.
Basement — 1,415 sq. ft.

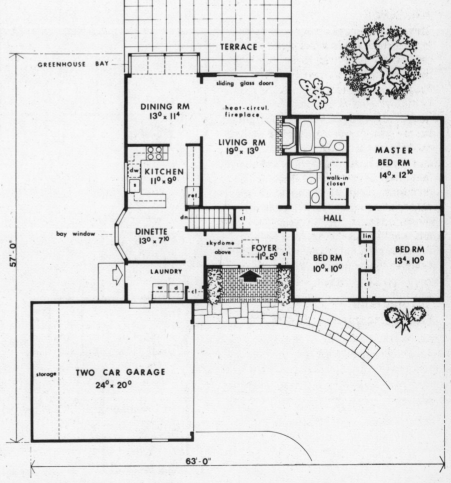

No. 90620

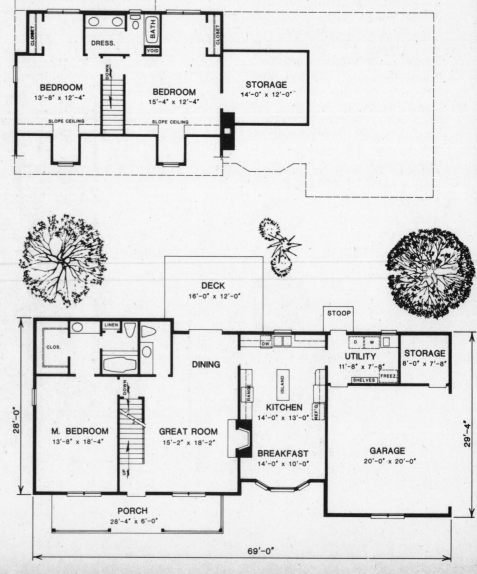

Country Living in a Doll House

No. 90410

Front porch, dormers, shutters and a bay window on the exterior of this rustic design are complemented by an informal interior. The main floor is divided into three sections. The eat-in country kitchen with island counter and bay window and a large utility room which can be entered from either the kitchen or garage. The second section is the great room with fireplace, an informal dining nook and double doors opening on to the rear deck or screened-in porch. The master suite features a walk-in closet and compartmentalized bath. The second floor consists of full bath and two bedrooms and a large storage room.

First floor — 1,277 sq. ft.
Second floor — 720 sq. ft.

Compact Home is Surprisingly Spacious

No. 90905

Searching for a design where the living room takes advantage of both front and rear views? Look no further. And, this cozy ranch has loads of other features. An attractive porch welcomes guests and provides shade for the big living room window on hot summer days. A large covered sundeck adjacent to the living room, dining room and kitchen will make entertaining a delight. The roomy bedrooms, including the master suite with full bath and a walk-in closet, are protected from street noise by the two-car garage.

Main floor — 1,314 sq. ft.
Unfinished basement — 1,488 sq. ft.
Garage — 484 sq. ft.
Width — 50 ft.
Depth — 54 ft.

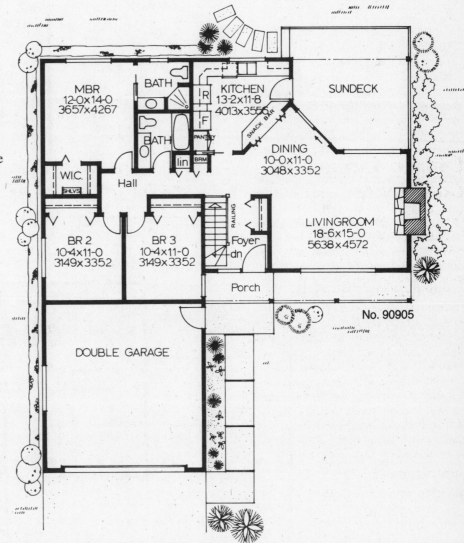

No. 90905

Traditional Design Enhanced by Open Loft

No. 90305

The sunken living room with its vaulted ceiling and fireplace provides a focal point for this lovely home. The master bedroom is on the main level, while two other bedrooms are situated on the upper level. The master bedroom has a separate vanity area just off the full-sized bath. The U-shaped kitchen is arranged for efficiency and convenience with direct access to the dining room, the patio and the garage. The upper level bedrooms with their large closets share a full bath and are separated by a loft, which serves to lend a feeling of openness and provide an additional area for relaxation.

Total area — 1,680 sq. ft.

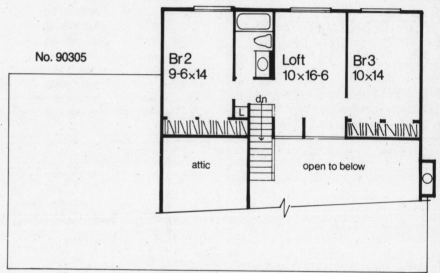

No. 90305

Br 2
9-6×14

Loft
10×16-6

Br 3
10×14

dn
L

attic

open to below

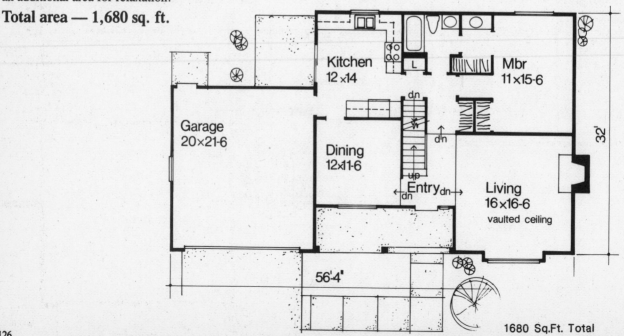

Garage
20×21-6

Kitchen
12×14

Mbr
11×15-6

Dining
12×11-6

dn

dn

up

Entry dn

Living
16×16-6
vaulted ceiling

32'

56'-4'

1680 Sq.Ft. Total

Split-Level Tudor Offers Comfort and Versatility

No. 10544

This contemporary Tudor-style design boasts features that make a house a home, including a master bedroom with a full bath, a spacious kitchen adjoining the formal dining room, and a fireplace in the large family room on the lower level. Steps up to the three bedrooms from the rest of the living areas gives the sense of privacy for family or guests. The bay window in the dining room provides a bit of elegance for entertaining.

Upper levels — 1,366 sq. ft.
Lower level - 384 sq. ft.
Basement - 631 sq. ft.
Garage - 528 sq. ft.

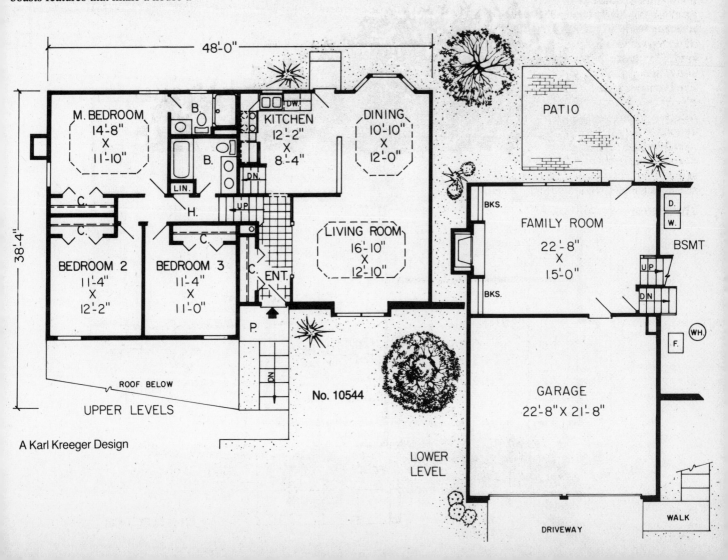

A Karl Kreeger Design

Good Things Come in Small Packages

No. 20303

Do you have a small lot, or a limited budget? Here's a compact gem that won't break the bank, and provides plenty of room for the whole family. And, this distinctive plan is an energy saver, too.

Look at the air-lock vestibule entry that keeps the chill outside, and the skylights in both baths that let the sun help with the heating bills. There's a cozy sitting nook in the living room. A matching nook off the kitchen is a perfect spot for family meals. To insure quiet bedtimes, the central staircase separates the downstairs bedrooms from active areas. But

for maximum privacy, escape upstairs to the master suite, which features double vanities, as well as a walk-in shower and tub.

First floor — 861 sq. ft.
Second floor — 333 sq. ft.
Basement — 715 sq. ft.

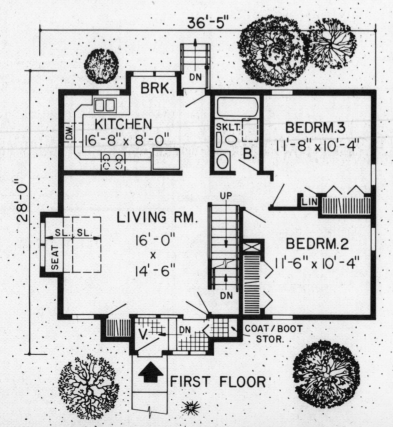

FIRST FLOOR

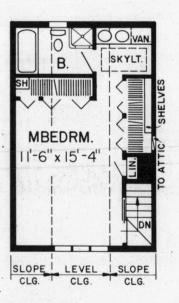

SECOND FLOOR

No. 20303

Glass Brings The Outdoors In

No. 9594

Adaptability is the outstanding characteristic of this modern two bedroom home. Imagine a folding partition wall that can enclose part of the expansive dining room to form a guest room or den. When the partitions are not in use, the living room and dining room, separated from the terrace only by sliding glass doors, offer an immense area for entertaining or relaxing. The kitchen is distinguished by an exposed brick wall which encloses the built-in oven.

First floor — 1,140 sq. ft.
Basement — 1,140 sq. ft.
Garage — 462 sq. ft.

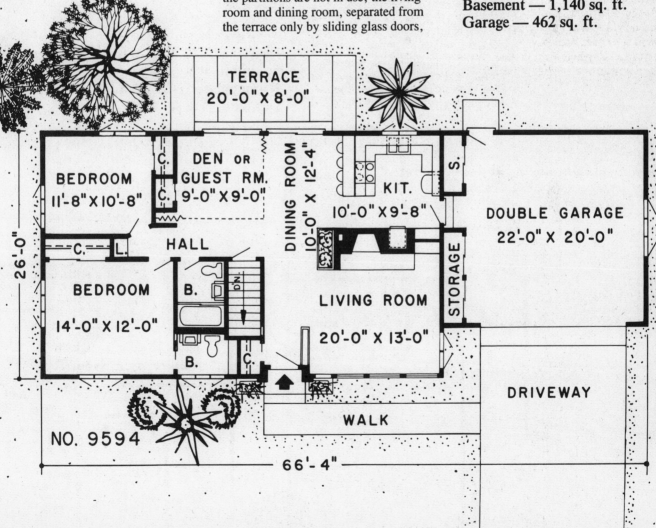

Built-In Beauty

No. 90942

The brick and stucco exterior of this beautiful home encloses a spacious plan designed for convenience. A huge, sunken living room with vaulted ceilings flows into the formal dining room overlooking the backyard Eat here, or in the nook on the other side of the adjoining kitchen. An open railing and a single stair separate the nook and the fireplaced family room, each featuring sliding glass doors to the patio. Notice the built-ins throughout the house that help keep clutter down, and the handy bath tucked behind the garage. Three bedrooms up the open staircase include the expansive master suite with private dressing room, walk-in closet, and double-vanitied bath with step-in shower.

First floor — 1,175 sq. ft.
Second floor — 776 sq. ft.
Basement — 1,165 sq. ft.
Garage — 410 sq. ft.

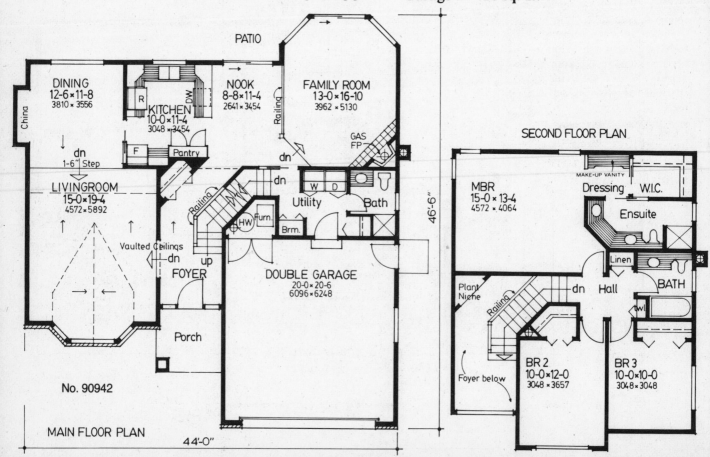

Year Round Retreat

No. 90613

This compact home is a bargain to build and designed to save on energy bills. Large glass areas face south, and the dramatic sloping ceiling of the living room allows heat from the wood-burning stove to rise into the upstairs bedrooms through high louvers on the inside wall. In hot weather, just open the windows on both floors for cooling air circulation. Sliding glass doors in the kitchen and living rooms open to the deck for outdoor dining or relaxation. One bedroom and a full bath complete the first floor. A stair off the foyer ends in a balcony with a commanding view of the living room. Two spacious bedrooms are separated by a full bath.

First floor — 917 sq. ft.
Second floor — 465 sq. ft.
(optional slab construction available)

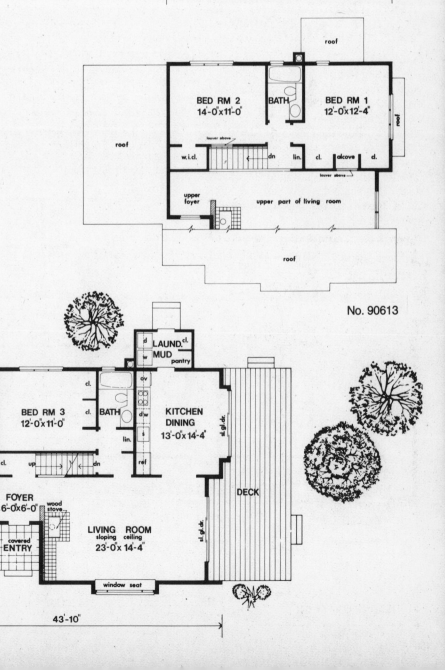

Greenhouse Brightens Compact Home

No. 20053

The kitchen features breakfast space, a built-in desk, pantry and a compact laundry area. Also on the first floor is the master bedroom with its private, five-piece bath. Both the entry foyer and the living room are open to the second floor creating a bridge between the two second floor bedrooms. In addition to the second floor's two bedrooms, full bath and linen closet, there is access to a large storage area under the eaves.

First floor — 1,088 sq. ft.
Second floor — 541 sq. ft.
Greenhouse — 72 sq. ft.
Garage — 473 sq. ft.

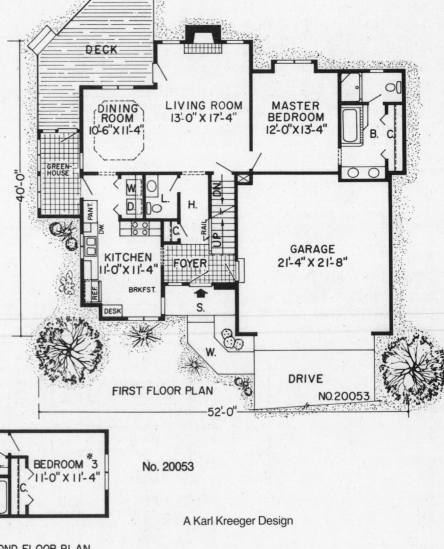

FIRST FLOOR PLAN

No. 20053

A Karl Kreeger Design

SECOND FLOOR PLAN

Compact Plan Allows For Gracious Living

No. 90158

A great room, accessible from the foyer, offers a cathedral ceiling with exposed beams, brick fireplace and access to the rear patio. The kitchen-breakfast area with center island and cathedral ceiling is accented by the round top window. The master bedroom has a full bath and walk-in closet. Two additional bedrooms and bath help make this an ideal plan for any growing family.

**First floor—1,540 sq. ft.
Basement—1,540 sq. ft.**

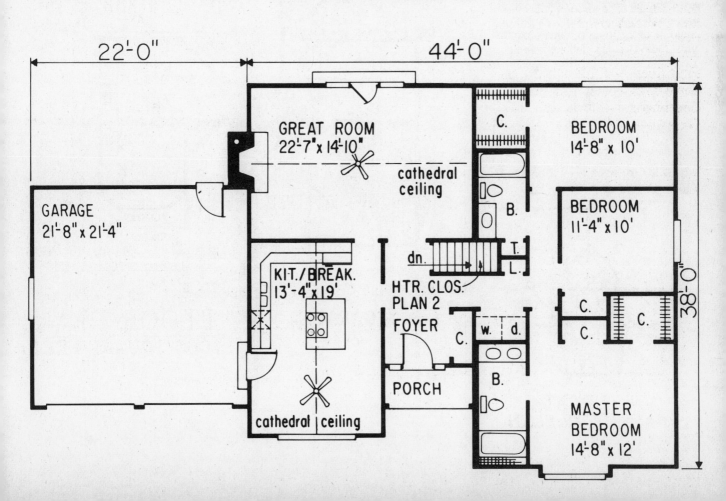

Carefree Comfort

No. 91418

Easy living awaits you in this one-level traditional designed with privacy in mind. A dramatic, vaulted foyer separates active areas from the three bedrooms. Down the skylit hall lies the master suite, where you'll discover the luxury of a private patio off the book-lined reading nook, decorative ceilings, and a well-appointed bath. The soaring roof line of the foyer continues into the great room, which combines with the bayed dining room to create a celebration of open space enhanced by abundant windows. The cook in the house will love the rangetop island kitchen and nook arrangement, loaded with storage inside, and surrounded by a built-in planter outside that's perfect for an herb garden.

**Main living area — 1,665 sq. ft.
Garage — 1-car**

ALTERNATE
BASEMENT PLAN

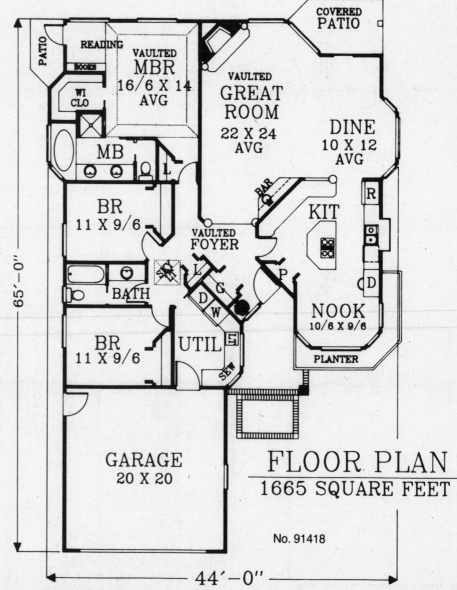

FLOOR PLAN
1665 SQUARE FEET

No. 91418

Comfortable Contemporary Design

No. 10567

This simple but well designed contemporary expresses comfort and offers a lot of options normally found in larger designs. On the first level, a front kitchen is offered with an open, non-partitioned dining area. Two bedrooms are located on the first floor. The living room sports a skylight, adding more natural lighting to the room, and has a prefabricated wood-burning fireplace. The second floor has a secluded master bedroom with a sitting room, walk-in closets, and a full bath. Other features include a two-car garage and a brick patio.

First floor — 1,046 sq. ft.
Second floor — 375 sq. ft.
Basement — 1,046 sq. ft.
Garage — 472 sq. ft.

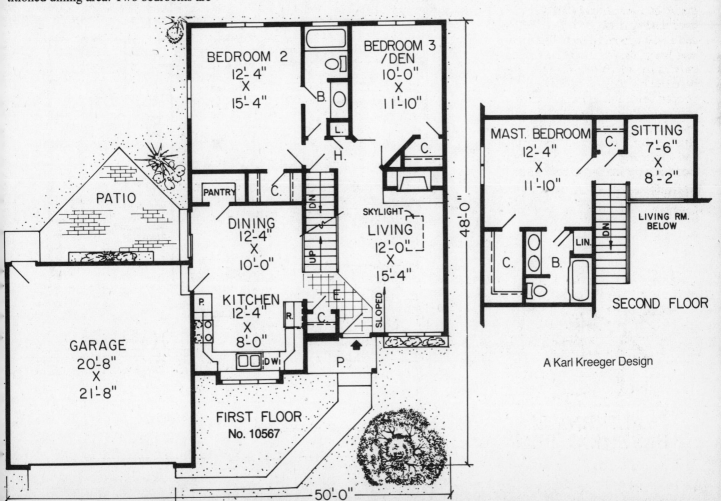

A Karl Kreeger Design

Outdoor-Lovers' Delight

No. 90248

If outdoor entertaining is your pleasure, this is the perfect house. Rain or shine, the covered porch off the dining room provides shelter, while the rear terrace lets you have fun in the sun. And, every room enjoys an outdoor atmosphere, thanks to sliding glass doors and over-sized windows. The well-appointed kitchen, centrally located just steps away from formal dinners, family suppers in the breakfast nook, or h'ors doeuvres in the soaring gathering room, is a cook's dream. Three bedrooms, tucked down a hall off the foyer, include the spacious master suite with its own private terrace access and full bath with step-in shower.

**Main living area — 1,729 sq. ft.
Garage — 2-car**

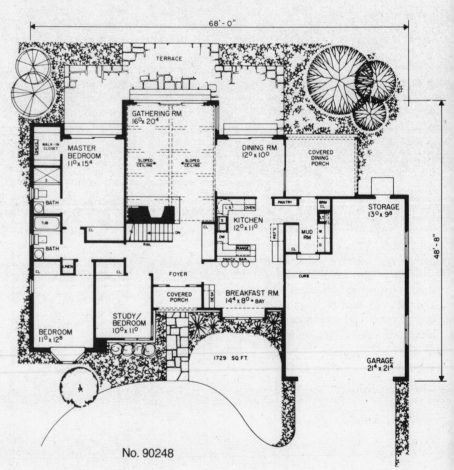

No. 90248

OPTIONAL NON-BASEMENT

Stately Home Features Formal Courtyard

No. 90014

Gracing the entrance of this elegant home is formal courtyard complete with reflecting pool. The grand foyer leads to the large living room which features a fireplace, window seats and an archway opening onto the dining room. The side terrace is easily reached through the dining room's French doors. The conveniently organized kitchen is located between the dining room and the family room, which is expanded by its French door entrances to both the front courtyard and the more informal porch. The three bedrooms located on the second floor are arranged to make the most efficient use of space.

First floor — 943 sq. ft.
Second floor — 772 sq. ft.

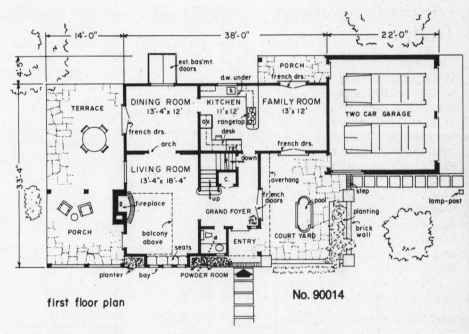

first floor plan   No. 90014

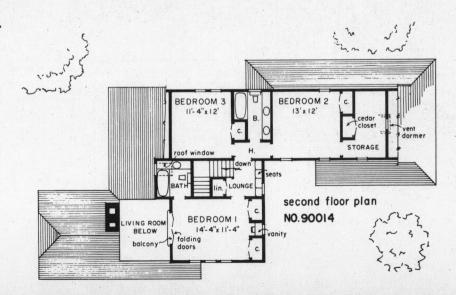

second floor plan
NO. 90014

Enjoy a Crackling Fire on a Chilly Day

No. 10683

From the dramatic, two-story entry to the full-length deck off the massive great room, this is a modern plan in a classic package. Cathedral ceilings soar over the formal dining and sunken living rooms, separated by an open railing. The corner kitchen efficiently serves formal and family eating areas. Can't you imagine a table overlooking the deck in the sunken great room's sunny bay? Up the angular staircase, two bedrooms, each with a huge closet, share a full bath. You'll have your own, private bath, including double vanities and a sun-washed raised tub, in the master suite at the rear of the house.

First floor — 990 sq. ft.
Second floor — 721 sq. ft.
Basement — 934 sq. ft.
Garage — 429 sq. ft.

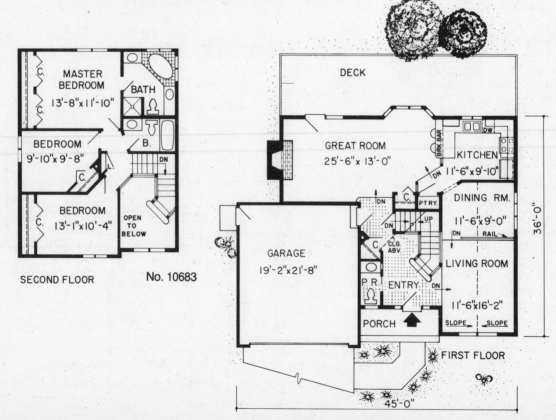

SECOND FLOOR   No. 10683

FIRST FLOOR

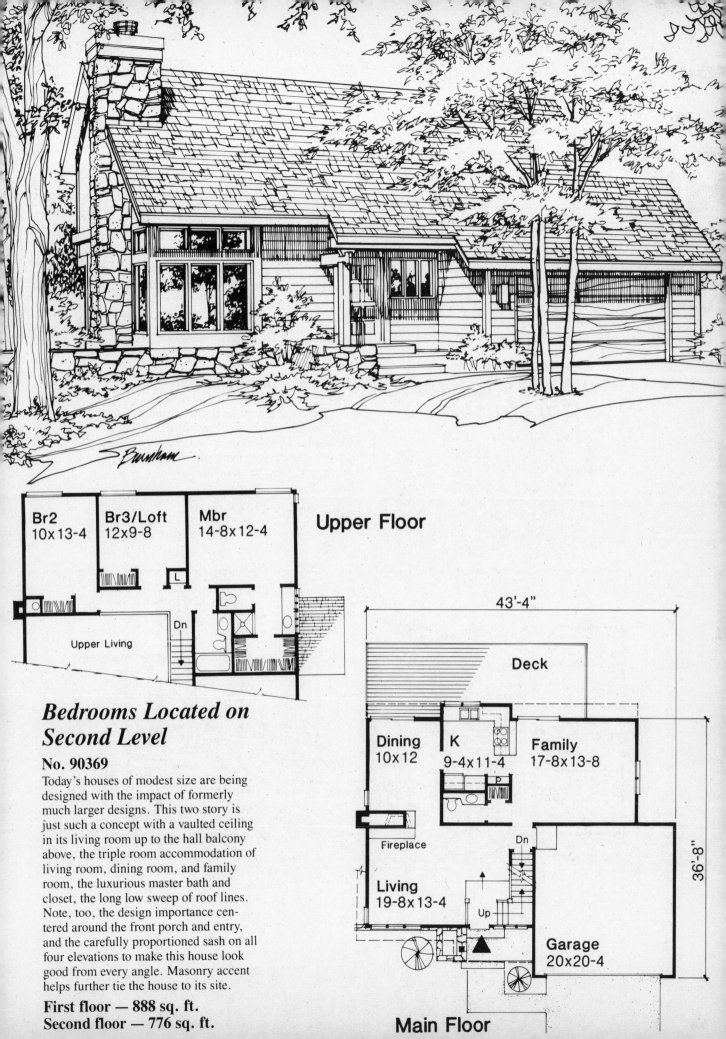

Upper Floor

Br2
10 x 13-4

Br3/Loft
12 x 9-8

Mbr
14-8 x 12-4

Upper Living

Dn

Bedrooms Located on Second Level

No. 90369

Today's houses of modest size are being designed with the impact of formerly much larger designs. This two story is just such a concept with a vaulted ceiling in its living room up to the hall balcony above, the triple room accommodation of living room, dining room, and family room, the luxurious master bath and closet, the long low sweep of roof lines. Note, too, the design importance centered around the front porch and entry, and the carefully proportioned sash on all four elevations to make this house look good from every angle. Masonry accent helps further tie the house to its site.

First floor — 888 sq. ft.
Second floor — 776 sq. ft.

43'-4"

Deck

Dining
10 x 12

K
9-4 x 11-4

Family
17-8 x 13-8

36'-8"

Fireplace

Dn

Living
19-8 x 13-4

Up

Garage
20 x 20-4

Main Floor

Western Approach To The Ranch House

No. 90007

Here is a house in authentic ranch style with long loggia, posts and braces, hand split shake roof, and cross-buck doors. Two wings sprawl at an angle on either side of a Texas-sized hexagonal living room. Directly across from the double-door entrance, a sunken living room is two steps lower and enhanced by two solid walls (one pierced by a fireplace), two 10' walls of almost solid glass (with sliding doors), and two walls opened wide as entrances from foyer and to dining room. For outdoor living and dining, a porch surrounds the room on three sides.

Living Area — 1,830 sq. ft.

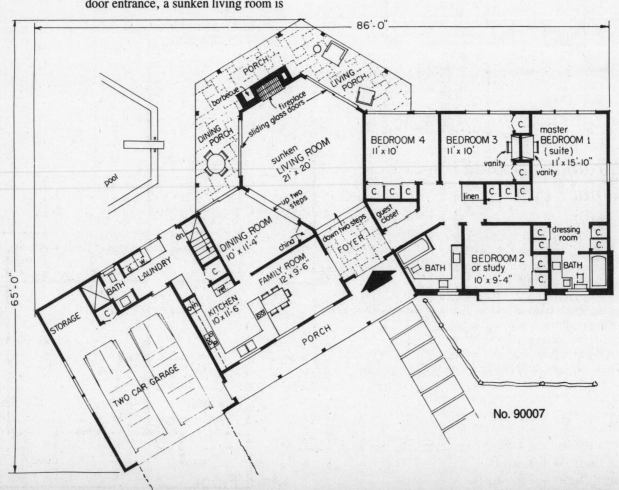

No. 90007

Cozy Cape Cod

No. 90115

This homey Cape home will blend beautifully in any setting. The formal living and dining rooms are completely separated from the family room, enabling adults and children to enjoy undisturbed everyday living. Notice the location of the first floor bath in relation to the din-ing room —a plan feature that permits this room to be used as a first floor bedroom, if desired. Back service entrance, mud room and laundry convenient to the kitchen are favorable points of the plan, too. On the second floor, the huge master bedroom has its own dressing area and entrance to the vanity bath.

First floor — 1,068 sq. ft.
Second floor — 804 sq. ft.

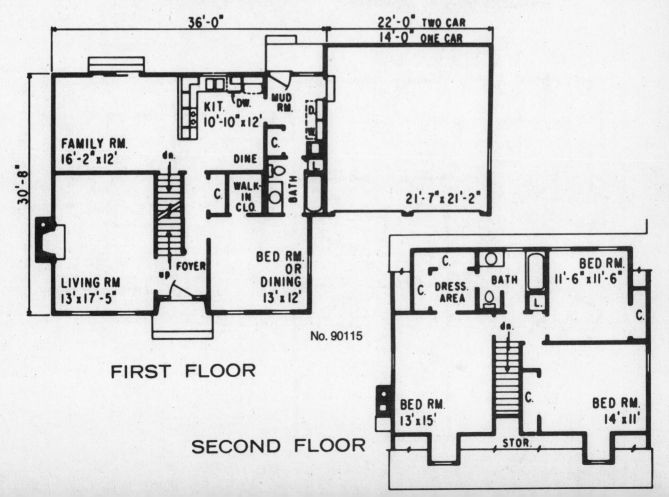

No. 90115

FIRST FLOOR

SECOND FLOOR

Multi-Level Living

No. 90837

You can enjoy a front and backyard view at the same time from the fireplaced living room of this traditional charmer. An open arrangement with the formal dining room makes it possible. A huge, bay window and sliders to the rear patio add an outdoor feeling to both rooms. Steps away, you'll find an efficient kitchen with a bayed nook overlooking the sunken family room. You could easily use the study off the family room as a guest room, with the handy lavatory just around the corner. Bedrooms are tucked upstairs, away from active areas. The master suite features a private bath and large double closet with mirrored doors. A hall bath serves the two front bedrooms.

First floor — 1,237 sq. ft.
Second floor — 605 sq. ft.
Basement — 601 sq. ft.
Garage — 420 sq. ft.

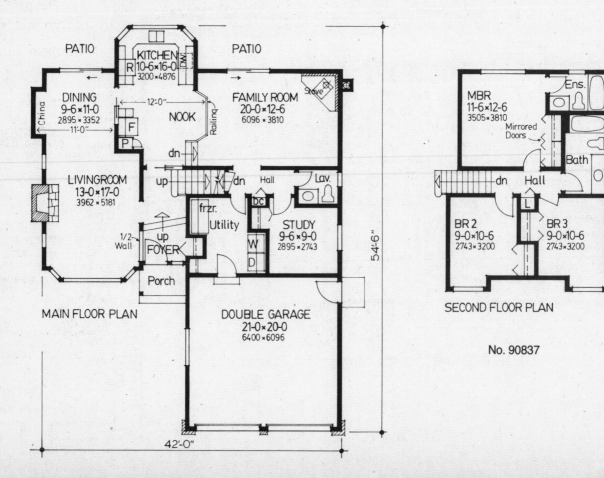

MAIN FLOOR PLAN

SECOND FLOOR PLAN

No. 90837

Fireplace Adds a Cozy Touch

No. 10760

Here's a handsome split-entry home that separates active and quiet areas. Step down to the garage level that includes a basement recreation and workshop area perfect for the household hobbyist. A short staircase leads up to the soaring living room, where the open feeling is accentuated by a huge bow window and a wide opening to the formal dining room. The kitchen lies behind swinging double doors, and features access to a raised rear deck. A few steps up, you'll find two full baths and three bedrooms with extra-large closets. Sloping ceilings add dramatic appeal to the private bedroom wing.

First floor — 1,676 sq. ft.
Basement recreation area — 592 sq. ft.
Workshop — 144 sq. ft.
Garage — 697 sq. ft.

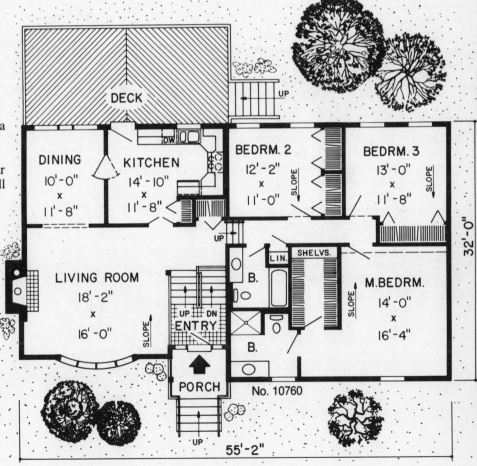

Bedrooms Flank Active Areas for Privacy

No. 20104

Hate to climb stairs? This one-level gem will accommodate your family in style, and keep your housework to a minimum. Recessed ceilings add an elegant touch to the dining room and master suite. And, with half walls, skylights, and a handy rear deck off the sunny breakfast room, there's an airy feeling throughout the centrally-located active areas. You'll appreciate the convenience of built-in storage in the kitchen and fireplaced living room, and the huge bedroom closets that keep the clutter down. Look at the private master bath with its twin vanities, raised tub and walk-in shower. Don't you deserve a little luxury?

Main living area — 1,686 sq. ft.
Basement — 1,677 sq. ft.
Garage — 475 sq. ft.

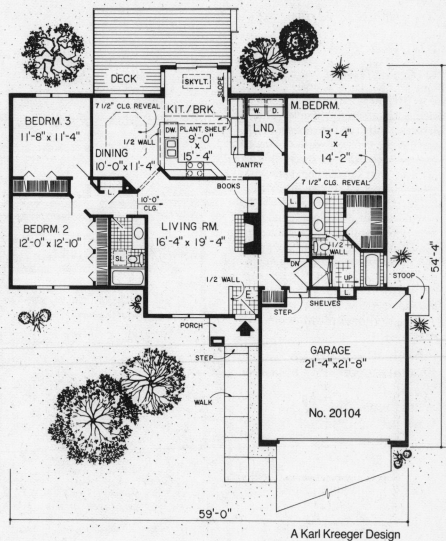

A Karl Kreeger Design

Suited to a Narrow Lot

No. 90814

If you need a compact home with room for all the kids, consider this traditional three bedroom plan. A large porch at the front door will provide ample protection from the weather. And, just inside the foyer the beautiful open stair will catch your eye. The island kitchen, nook and sunken family room create a spacious and comfortable family living and work space. A few short steps away, you'll find a convenient utility area with adjacent powder room.

Main floor — 1,080 sq. ft.
Second floor — 761 sq. ft.
Garage — 420 sq. ft.
Unfinished basement — 1,067 sq. ft.

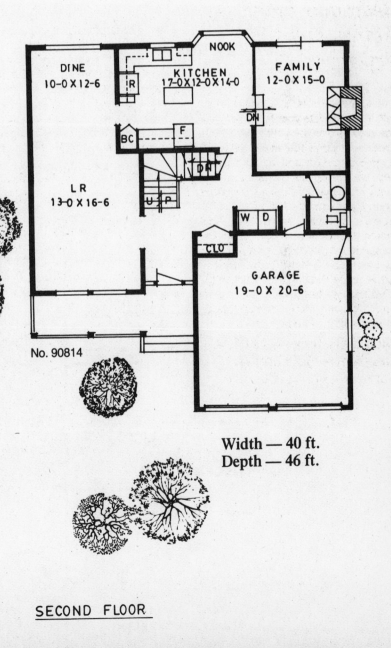

No. 90814

DINE 10-0 X 12-6
NOOK
KITCHEN 17-0 X 12-0 X 14-0
FAMILY 12-0 X 15-0
R
BC
F
DN
LR 13-0 X 16-6
UP
DN
W D
CLO
GARAGE 19-0 X 20-6

Width — 40 ft.
Depth — 46 ft.

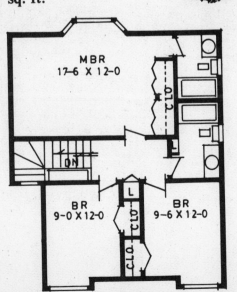

MBR 17-6 X 12-0
CLO
DN
BR 9-0 X 12-0
CLO
BR 9-6 X 12-0

SECOND FLOOR

Open Plan Accented by Loft, Windows and Decks

No. 10515

The first floor living space of this inviting home blends the family room and dining room for comfortable family living. The large kitchen shares a preparation/eating bar with the dining room. The ample utility room is designed with a pantry plus room for a freezer, washer and dryer. Also on the first floor is the master suite with its two closets and five piece bath which opens into a greenhouse. The second floor is highlighted by a loft which overlooks the first floor living area. The two upstairs bedrooms each have double closets and share a four-piece, compartmentalized bath.

First floor — 1,280 sq. ft.
Second floor — 735 sq. ft.
Greenhouse — 80 sq. ft.
Playhouse — 80 sq. ft.

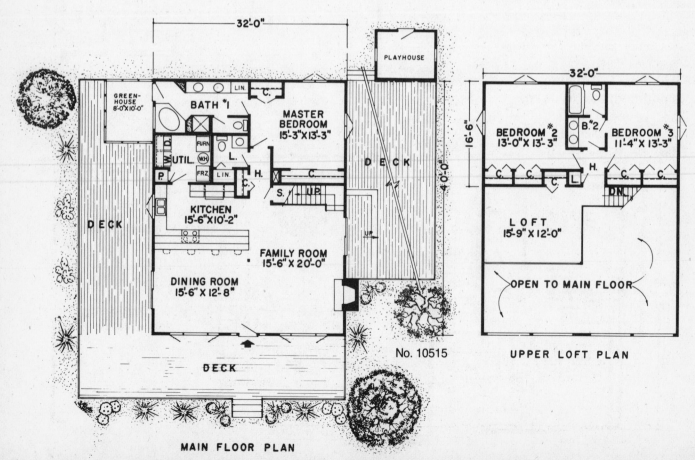

MAIN FLOOR PLAN

No. 10515

UPPER LOFT PLAN

Inviting Porch Adorns Affordable Home

No. 90682

You don't have to give up storage space to build an affordable home. With large closets just inside the front door and in every bedroom, a walk-in pantry by the kitchen, and an extra-large storage area tucked behind the garage, you can build this house on an optional slab foundation and still keep the clutter to a minimum. The L-shaped living and dining room arrangement, brightened by triple windows and sliding glass doors, adds a spacious feeling to active areas. Eat in formal elegance overlooking the patio, or have a family meal in the country kitchen. Tucked in a private wing for a quiet bedtime atmosphere, three bedrooms and two full baths complete this affordable home loaded with amenities.

Living area — 1,160 sq. ft.
Garage — 2-car

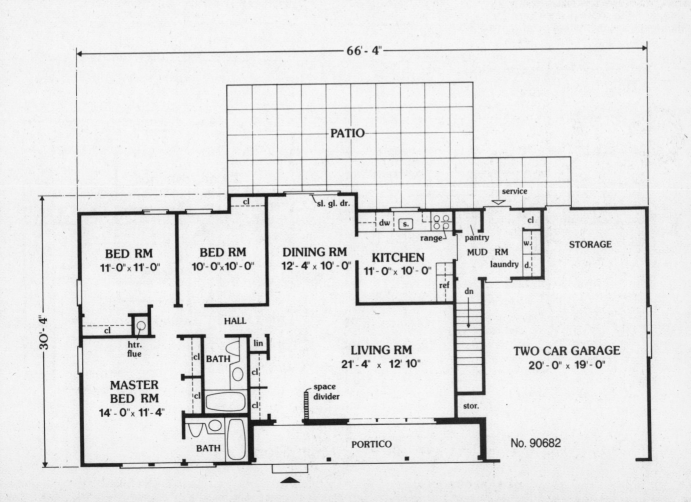

No. 90682

Country Classic Full of Character

No. 90397

Towering gables softened by gentle arches add old-fashioned charm to this tidy, three-bedroom traditional. But, look at the updated interior. Corner transom windows create a sunny atmosphere throughout the open plan. A fireplace divides the vaulted living room and dining room, contributing to the spacious, yet warm feeling in this inviting home. Any cook would envy the efficient layout of the country kitchen, with its corner sink overlooking the deck and family sitting area. And, even your plants will enjoy the greenhouse atmosphere of the vaulted master suite, which features a double-vanitied bath and walk-in closet. Another full bath serves the children's rooms.

First floor — 834 sq. ft.
Second floor — 722 sq. ft.
Garage — 2-car

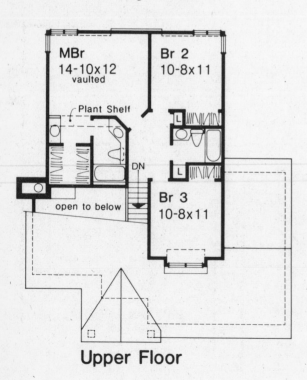

Upper Floor

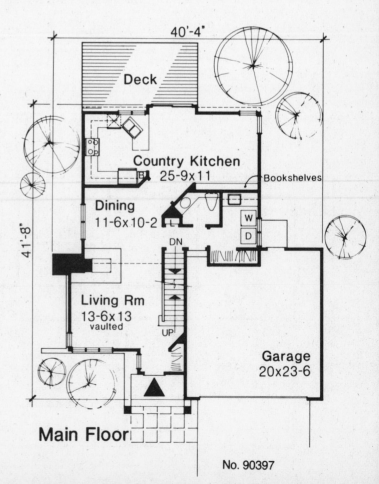

Main Floor

No. 90397

Private Places

No. 90563

The central entry does more than just
welcome guests to this spacious, one-
level home; it separates active and quiet
areas for privacy. In the bedroom wing,
you'll find three bedrooms and two full
baths. The master suite is a special treat,
with its huge, walk-in closet, double vanities, separate toilet area, and jacuzzi tub.
The living and dining rooms open to the
entry for a wide-open feeling accentuated
by towering windows and high ceilings.
And, overlooking the backyard, the
kitchen of your dreams features a cooktop island, a bayed breakfast nook, and
an adjoining family room complete with
a cozy fireplace.

Main living area — 1,990 sq. ft.
Garage — 2-car

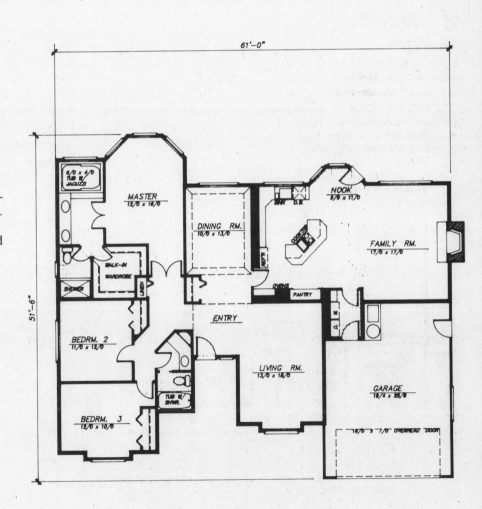

No. 90563

Formal Balance

No. 90689

Here's a magnificent example of classical design with a contemporary twist. The graceful columns that adorn the facade of this one-level beauty separate interior spaces without walls. And, combined with the half-round windows in the living room, they create an open, elegant feeling throughout formal areas. A bow window in the dining room overlooking the deck echoes the classic image. Kitchen and dinette share the open atmosphere, flowing together into a spacious unit that opens to the rear deck through sliding glass doors. The master suite enjoys a private corner of the deck, complete with hot-tub, double-vanitied bath, and ample closets. Two front-facing bedrooms across the hall share another full bath.

**Main living area — 1,374 sq. ft.
Basement — 1,361 sq. ft.
Mudroom-laundry — 102 sq. ft.
Garage — 548 sq. ft.**

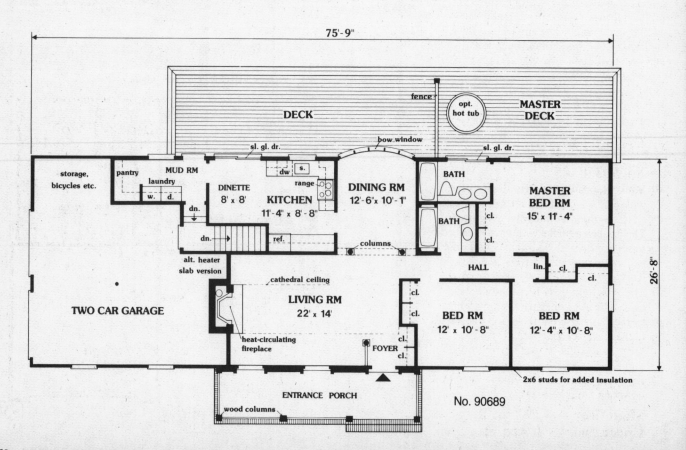

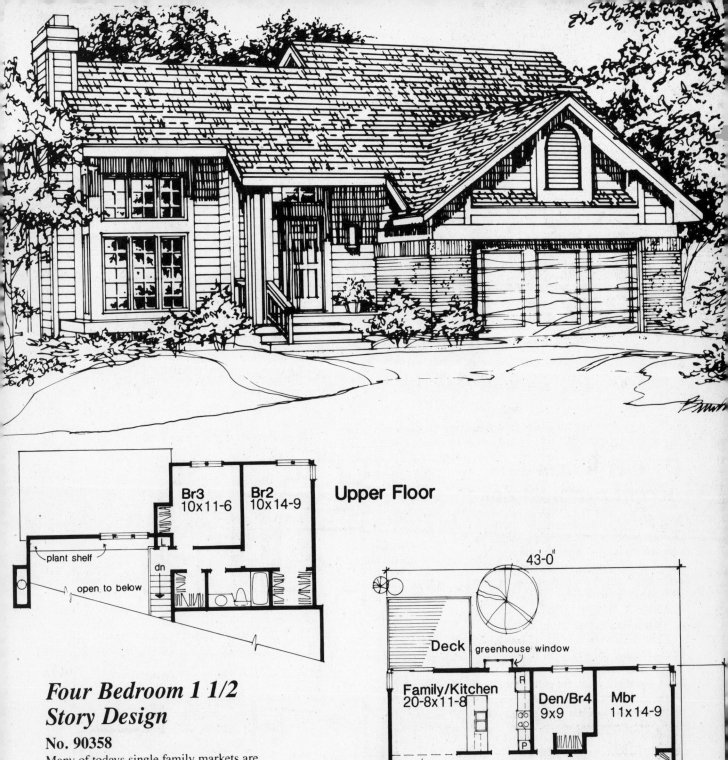

Upper Floor

Br3
10x11-6

Br2
10x14-9

plant shelf

open to below

dn

Four Bedroom 1 1/2 Story Design

No. 90358

Many of todays single family markets are looking for a flexible plan that grows and adapts to their families changing needs. This is such a house with its master bedroom and den/4th bedroom down, double bedrooms up, stacked baths and well working open and flowing living areas. The exterior impact is of hi-style, hi-value; the interior impact is highlighted by the vaulted living room and thru views to the rear deck and yard. This house belongs in a neighborhood where the custom exterior look will make for a surprising space/value combination to the move up young family market.

Main floor — 1,062 sq. ft.
Upper floor — 469 sq. ft.

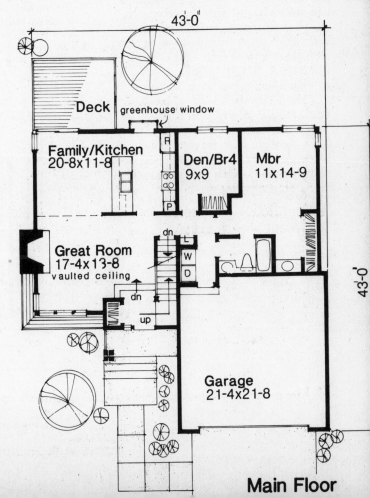

43'-0"

Deck   greenhouse window

Family/Kitchen
20-8x11-8

Den/Br4
9x9

Mbr
11x14-9

Great Room
17-4x13-8
vaulted ceiling

dn

up

W
D

43'-0"

Garage
21-4x21-8

Main Floor

Dormer Windows
Accent Bedroom Zone

No. 5035

Dormer windows, shutters and faithfully
detailed traditional entry combine to create a unique appeal in this Cape Cod
offering. Perhaps the easiest way to zone
sleeping areas is to place bedrooms on
a another floor, and, in this case, the
result is a substantial master bedroom
and two smaller bedrooms, all provided
with adequate closet space. Below, the
living room reaches a full 22 feet to
allow plenty of room for entertaining and
borders a handy half bath. Swinging
doors separate kitchen and dining room.

First floor — 726 sq.ft.
Second floor — 622 sq.ft.
Basement — 726 sq.ft.

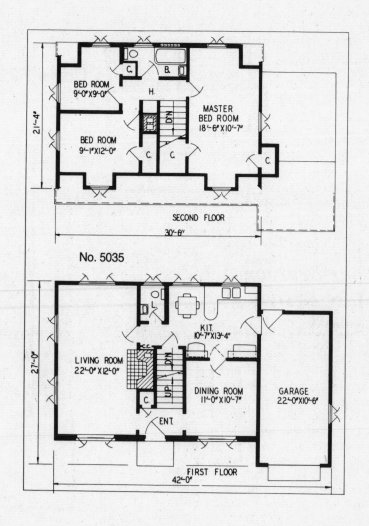

SECOND FLOOR
30'-6"

No. 5035

FIRST FLOOR
42'-0"

Compact Design for a Small Lot

No. 10597

Sloping ceilings and a corner fireplace distinguish the living room of this cozy three bedroom home. Eat in the formal dining room with recessed ceiling or in the roomy kitchen, which features sliding glass doors to the patio. Walk by the laundry and pantry to the master bedroom suite. Upstairs, two bedrooms share a bath with double sinks.

First floor — 1,162 sq. ft.
Second floor — 464 sq. ft.
Basement — 1,118 sq. ft.
Garage — 450 sq. ft.

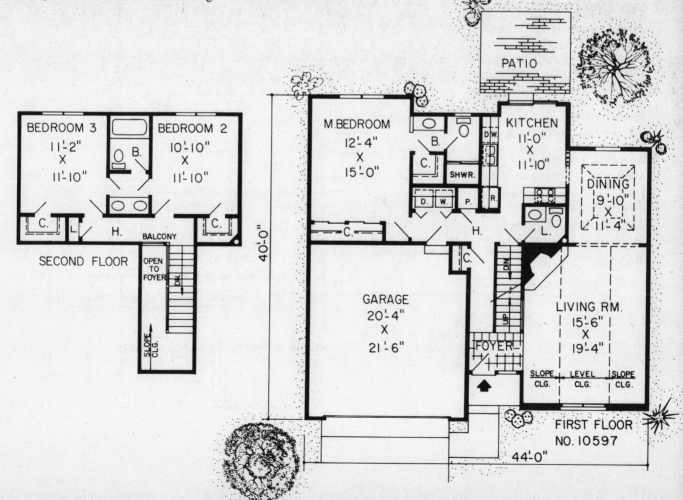

Compact Charmer Flooded with Sun

No. 20300

The clerestory window high over the covered porch of this inviting gem hints at the high excitement you'll find when you walk through the front door. From the soaring foyer to the sun room off the fireplaced living room and kitchen, this contemporary porch revival house is enveloped in warmth and sunlight. And, you'll find all the features you've been longing for: built in media and china cabinets, an efficient U-shaped kitchen, a central yet concealed first-floor powder room, a skylit master bath with double vanities, and three spacious bedrooms with loads of closet space.

First floor — 909 sq. ft.
Second floor — 765 sq. ft.
Basement — 517 sq. ft.
Garage and stair — 479 sq. ft.

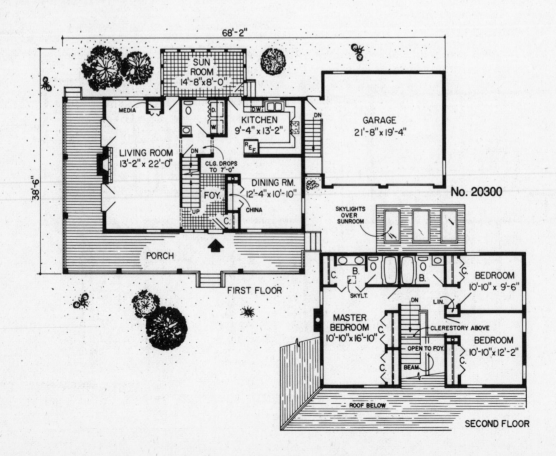

Open Plan Features Great Room and Exterior Options

No. 90328

With a skylight and a vaulted ceiling, the great room will welcome family and guests alike. This inviting room also includes a fireplace, sliding door access to the deck and a wet bar. The roomy eat-in kitchen features an efficient U-shaped work area and lots of windows in the dining area. The three bedrooms and two full baths incorporate unusual angled entries so as to make the most of every foot of floor space. The master bedroom combines its bath and dressing area. The third bedroom would make a cozy den or a handy room for guests.

Main floor — 1,400 sq. ft.
Basement — 1,350 sq. ft.
Garage — 374 sq. ft.

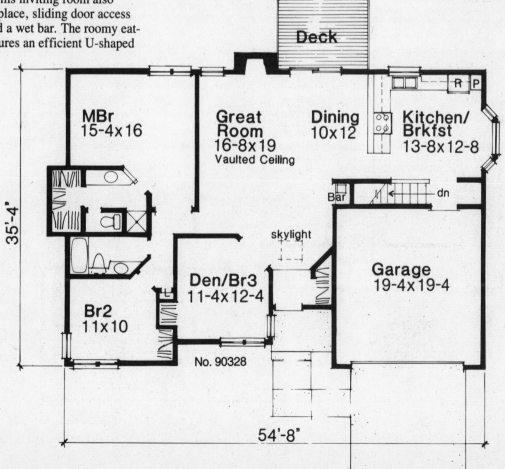

Deck

MBr 15-4x16

Great Room 16-8x19 Vaulted Ceiling

Dining 10x12

Kitchen/ Brkfst 13-8x12-8

R P

Bar

dn

skylight

Den/Br3 11-4x12-4

Garage 19-4x19-4

Br2 11x10

No. 90328

35'-4"

54'-8"

High Impact on a Low Budget

No. 10742

Build this Spanish-style, three bedroom gem on a slab to keep costs down and interest high. A trio of arches graces the porch of this one-level home, and provides a warm welcome to entering guests. Inside, dramatic cathedral ceilings bring an exciting atmosphere to the open living room, separated from the foyer by a half-wall, and warmed by a fireplace that dominates one wall. Soaring ceilings at the rear of the house are pierced by a skylight, bathing the dining room and island kitchen in warmth and light. The adjoining patio, accessible from the dining room and master suite, is a perfect spot to enjoy your first cup of coffee on a beautiful summer morning.

Main living area — 1,617 sq. ft.
Garage — 528 sq. ft.

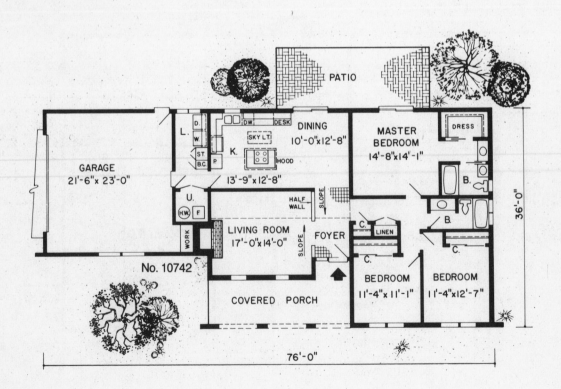

Lattice Trim Adds Nostalgic Charm

No. 99315

Thanks to vaulted ceilings and an ingenious plan, this wood and fieldstone classic feels much larger than its compact size. The entry, dominated by a skylit staircase to the bedroom floor, opens to the vaulted living room with a balcony view and floor-to-ceiling corner window treatment. Eat in the spacious, formal dining room, in the sunny breakfast nook off the kitchen, or, when the weather's nice, out on the adjoining deck. Pass-through convenience makes meal service easy wherever you choose to dine. A full bath at the top of the stairs serves the kids' bedrooms off the balcony hall. But, the master suite boasts its own, private bath, along with a private dressing area.

First floor — 668 sq. ft.
Second floor — 691 sq. ft.
Garage — 2-car

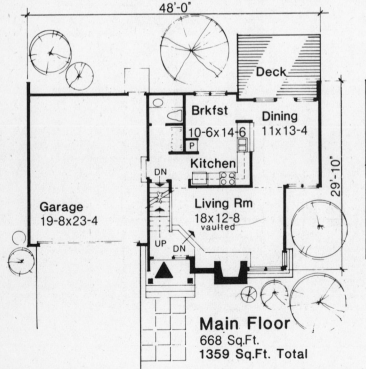

Main Floor
668 Sq.Ft.
1359 Sq.Ft. Total

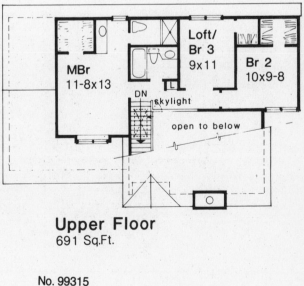

Upper Floor
691 Sq.Ft.

No. 99315

Convertible Charm

No. 91500

The compact footprint of this three-bedroom charmer makes it an ideal choice for the homebuilder on a budget, but its wide-open plan keeps the walls from closing in. Step inside the entry to a dramatic living and dining room that rises two stories. The living room fireplace adds a cozy feeling to both rooms. At the rear of the house, you'll find a well-appointed kitchen convenient to both dining and family rooms. Upstairs, three bedrooms and two baths feature ample closet space and intriguing shapes that offer great decorating possibilities. The master suite is especially inviting, with its vaulted ceiling, double-vanitied bath, and huge window overlooking the backyard.

First floor — 748 sq. ft.
Second floor — 720 sq. ft.
Garage — 2-car

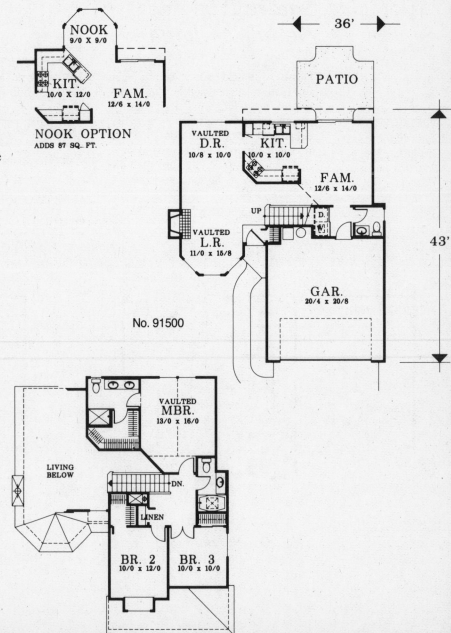

NOOK
9/0 X 9/0

KIT.
10/0 X 12/0

FAM.
12/6 x 14/0

NOOK OPTION
ADDS 87 SQ. FT.

36'

PATIO

VAULTED
D.R.
10/8 x 10/0

KIT.
10/0 x 10/0

FAM.
12/6 x 14/0

VAULTED
L.R.
11/0 x 15/8

UP

43'

GAR.
20/4 x 20/8

No. 91500

VAULTED
MBR.
13/0 x 16/0

LIVING
BELOW

DN.

LINEN

BR. 2
10/0 x 12/0

BR. 3
10/0 x 10/0

Affordable Amenities

No. 10794

This home offers convenience, charm, and the amenities you've been looking for, in an attractive plan that's won't break your building budget. Look at all the features that make life easier: one-floor living for easy cleaning, a large, built-in pantry off the dining room, an efficient U-shaped kitchen, a separate laundry, and handy garage entry. And the special touches — like a private bath in the corner master suite, another hall bath that serves the two back bedrooms, and sliding glass doors that brighten the dining room adjoining the spacious living room, make this a home your family will cherish for years to come.

Main living area — 1,400 sq. ft.
Optional garage — 528 sq. ft.

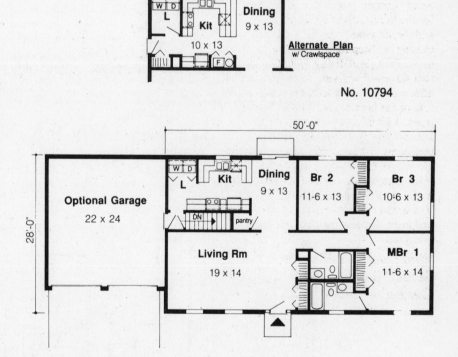

Built-Ins Add Extra Storage Space

No. 90207

This versatile, one-level plan keeps active and quiet areas separate for maximum privacy. A massive fireplace with raised hearth divides the central entry from the huge gathering room. Notice how common areas flow together. Three sliding doors off the gathering and dining rooms and the glass walls of the bayed breakfast nook combine with this open arrangement to create a spacious feeling throughout the area. Need warm weather living space? Retreat to the surrounding rear terrace for stargazing or a candlelit dinner. A hallway tucked off the entry leads to three bedrooms and two full baths. You'll appreciate the generous closet space and the private terrace access in the master suite.

**Living area — 1,366 sq. ft.
Garage — 2-car**

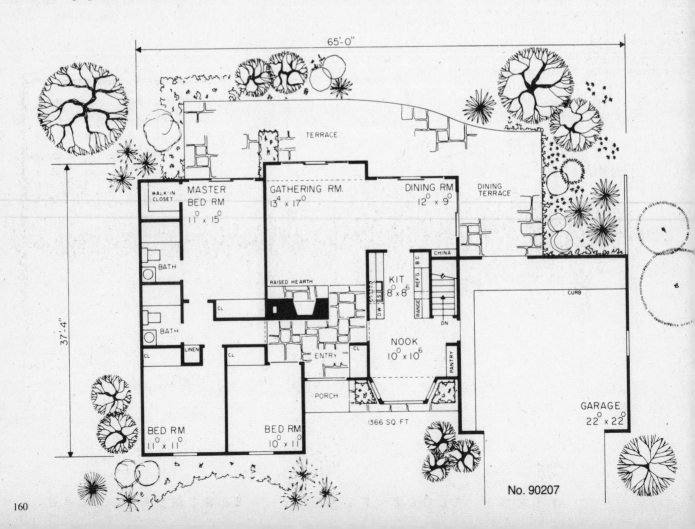

No. 90207

Rustic Design Blends with Hillside

No. 10012
Naturally perfect for a woodland setting, this redwood decked home will adapt equally well to a lake or ocean setting. A car or boat garage is furnished on the lower level. Fireplaces equip both the living room and the 36-foot long family room which opens onto a shaded patio. A laundry room adjoins the open kitchen which shares the large redwood deck encircling the living and dining area. Two bedrooms and two full baths on the first floor supplement another bedroom and half bath on the lower level.

First floor — 1,198 sq. ft.
Basement — 1,198 sq. ft.

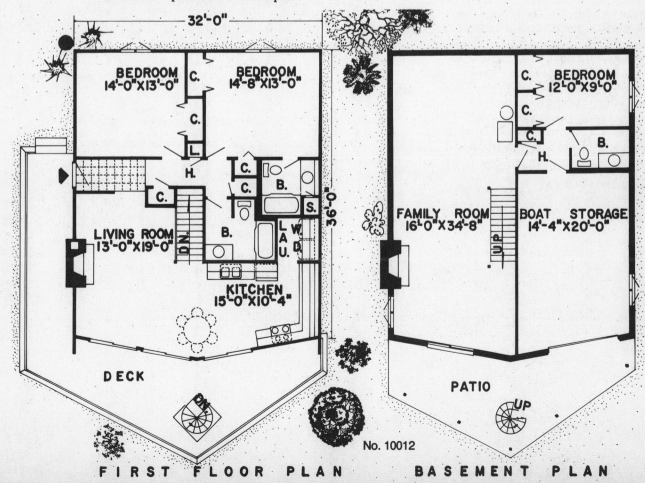

FIRST FLOOR PLAN   BASEMENT PLAN

No. 10012

Privacy Zones

No. 91506

Do you want one-level living without compromising your privacy? Here's a home that will house your family in easy-care elegance, with bedrooms tucked away from the bustle of active areas. The central foyer opens to a large living and dining room combination brightened by a sun-catching bay window. At the rear of the house, an open plan allows the fireplace in the family room to spread its warmth through the angular, efficient kitchen and cheerful nook with sliders to the rear patio. A hallway off the foyer leads to the three bedrooms, laundry room, and handy garage entry. A hall bath serves the kids' rooms, but the master suite features its own private bath with step-in shower.

Main living area — 1,546 sq. ft.
Garage — 2-car

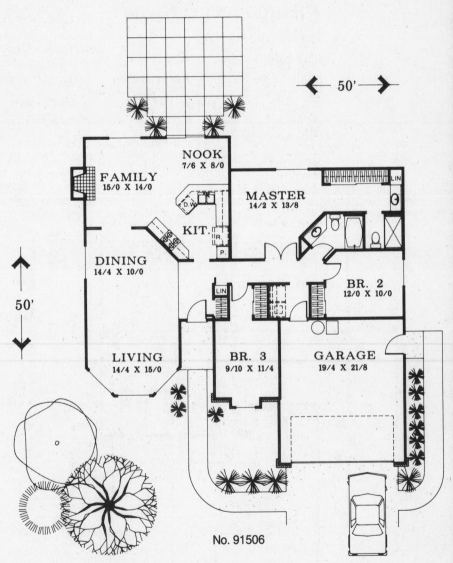

← 50' →

50'

NOOK
7/6 X 8/0

FAMILY
15/0 X 14/0

MASTER
14/2 X 13/8

KIT.

DINING
14/4 X 10/0

BR. 2
12/0 X 10/0

LIVING
14/4 X 15/0

BR. 3
9/10 X 11/4

GARAGE
19/4 X 21/8

No. 91506

Compact Cost-Saver

No. 10795

It's hard to find a home that gets this much living space into such a compact package. And its simple foundation plan will keep your construction costs at a manageable level. A covered porch shelters guests who enter the huge living room inside the front door, which feels even more spacious with its open arrangement with the dining room overlooking the backyard. Just steps away, the efficient galley kitchen shares the backyard view. You'll appreciate the extra storage space in the adjoining laundry room, and in the pantry off the dining room. Past the basement stairway, a hallway leads to the quiet wing, where four bedrooms and two full baths mean the morning rush will be just a little easier.

Main living area — 1,534 sq. ft.
Optional garage — 440 sq. ft.

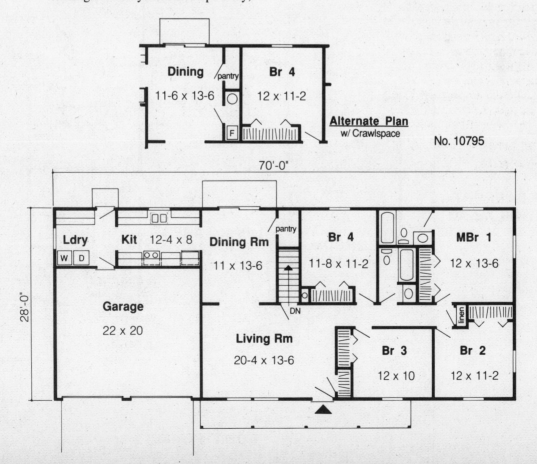

Design Features Six Ideas

No. 1074

Simple lines flow from this six-sided design. It's affordably scaled, but sizable enough for a growing family. Active living areas are snuggled centrally between two quiet bedroom and bath areas in the floor plan. A small hallway, leading to two bedrooms and a full bath on the right side, may be completely shut off from the living room, providing seclusion. Another bath lies behind a third bedroom on the left side, complete with washer-dryer facilities and close enough to a stoop and rear entrance to serve as a mudroom.

First floor — 1,040 sq. ft.
Storage — 44 sq. ft.
Deck — 258 sq. ft.
Carport — 230 sq. ft.

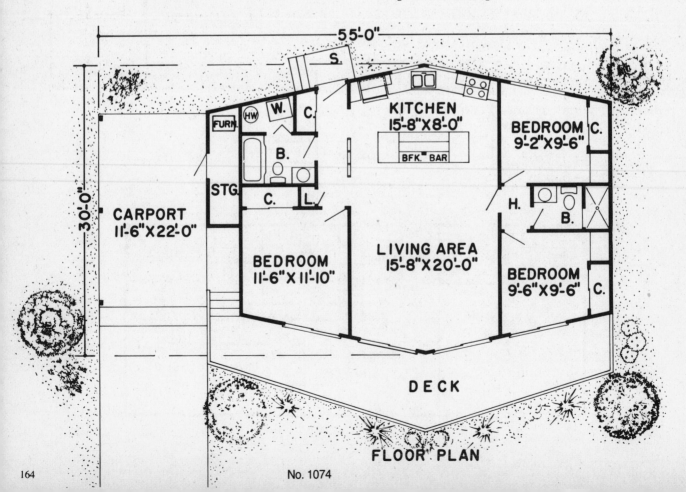

FLOOR PLAN

Save Three Ways

No. 10792

Here's a handsome, clapboard charmer that offers lots of options for keeping building costs down. This home's simple foundation keeps your budget in check, but you can cut costs even more by eliminating the garage, and using the alternate crawlspace instead of the full basement plan. Whatever your choice, you'll still enjoy the cozy atmosphere of the formal living and dining rooms that flank the entry. And you'll love the convenient, U-shaped kitchen just steps away. Tucked down a hall, the three bedrooms are served by a handy full bath. Notice the huge, walk-in closet in the master bedroom.

Main living area — 1,204 sq. ft.
Optional garage — 560 sq. ft.

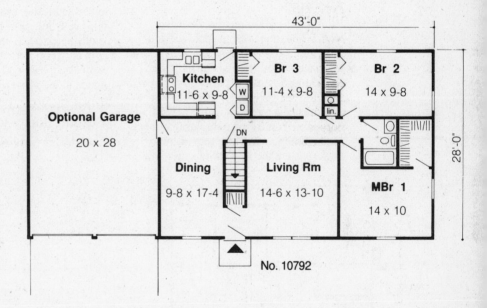

43'-0"

28'-0"

Optional Garage
20 x 28

Kitchen
11-6 x 9-8

W
D

Br 3
11-4 x 9-8

lin.

Br 2
14 x 9-8

DN

Dining
9-8 x 17-4

Living Rm
14-6 x 13-10

MBr 1
14 x 10

No. 10792

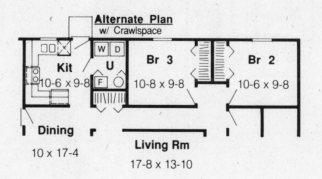

Alternate Plan
w/ Crawlspace

W D

U

Kit
10-6 x 9-8

F

Br 3
10-8 x 9-8

Br 2
10-6 x 9-8

Dining
10 x 17-4

Living Rm
17-8 x 13-10

Family Plan

No. 91504

With four bedrooms and a wealth of open space, this home is ideal for your growing family. The two-story foyer sets the stage for the spacious feeling you'll find throughout the house. Formal areas flow together in a sunny arrangement accentuated by a bay window in the living room. You'll find a similar treatment in the family areas at the rear of the house, where the island kitchen, break-fast nook, and family room all benefit from a vaulted ceiling crowned by a fire-place and lots of windows overlooking the backyard. Four bedrooms and two baths lie up the L-shaped staircase that ascends from the foyer. Notice the elegant skylit bath and generous closet space in the master suite.

First floor — 1,105 sq. ft.
Second floor — 950 sq. ft.
Garage — 2-car

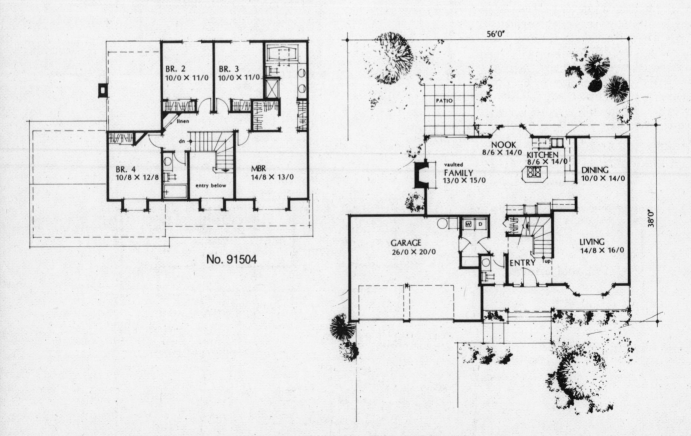

No. 91504

Built-In Options

No. 10796

Vertical siding adds a contemporary flavor to this one-level home, where a simple footprint means super savings on foundation costs. The central entry tucked under the eave opens three ways: to the private bedroom wing on the right, straight ahead into the massive great room overlooking the backyard, and left into the front-facing kitchen. You'll love the convenience the U-shaped kitchen offers, with its built-in pantry, and location just across the counter from the dining room. Notice the amenities in the rear-facing master suite, including huge his and hers closets and a private bath. Another full bath serves the front bedrooms. The laundry location is a step-saver you're sure to appreciate.

Main living area — 1,644 sq. ft.
Optional garage — 576 sq. ft.

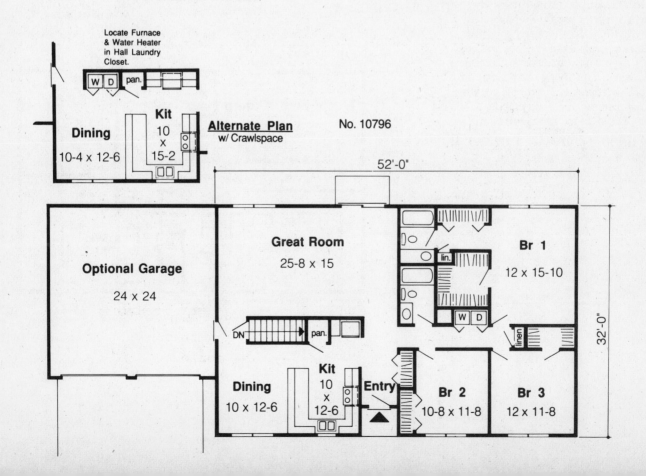

Locate Furnace & Water Heater in Hall Laundry Closet.

W D pan.

Dining 10-4 x 12-6

Kit 10 x 15-2

Alternate Plan w/ Crawlspace

No. 10796

52'-0"

Optional Garage 24 x 24

Great Room 25-8 x 15

lin.

Br 1 12 x 15-10

W D

linen

DN pan.

Dining 10 x 12-6

Kit 10 x 12-6

Entry

Br 2 10-8 x 11-8

Br 3 12 x 11-8

32'-0"

Super Starter

No. 10791

This affordable plan will let you have your house now, and keep your building budget in check. The entry opens to a spacious living room brightenened by a triple window arrangement. Step back to an open kitchen and dining room combination that features sliding glass doors to the backyard. The side entry, opposite the basement stairway, is handy when the kids come in from an afternoon of play. Prefer to save on foundation costs? Build the alternate crawlspace plan and separate the kitchen and breakfast nook with counters and cabinets. A hallway off the living room keeps the three bedrooms away from the action. Each features ample closet space, and easy access to the large, hall bath.

Main living area — 1,092 sq. ft.

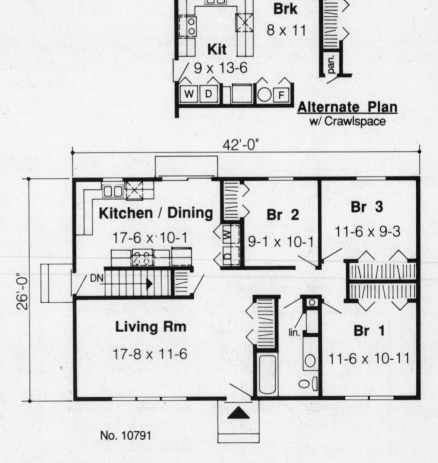

Brk
8 x 11

Kit
9 x 13-6

Alternate Plan
w/ Crawlspace

42'-0"

Kitchen / Dining
17-6 x 10-1

Br 2
9-1 x 10-1

Br 3
11-6 x 9-3

26'-0"

DN

Living Rm
17-8 x 11-6

lin.

Br 1
11-6 x 10-11

No. 10791

Vacation Retreat Suits Year-round Living

No. 1078

A long central hallway divides formal from informal areas, assuring privacy for the two bedrooms located in the rear. Also located along the central portion of the design are a utility room and a neighboring bath. The furnace, water heater and washer-dryer units are housed in the utility room. An open living/dining room area with exposed beams, sloping ceilings and optional fireplace occupies the front. Two pairs of sliding glass doors access the large deck from this area. The house may also be entered from the carport on the right or the deck on the left.

First floor — 1,024 sq. ft.
Carport & storage — 387 sq. ft.
Deck — 411 sq. ft.

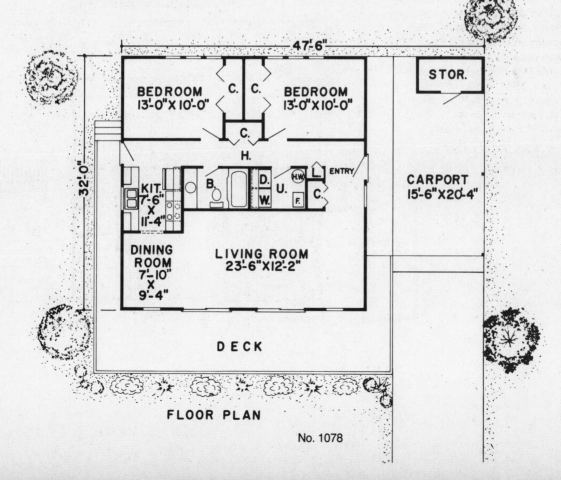

FLOOR PLAN

No. 1078

Three Levels of Spacious Living

No. 10396

This passive solar design is suitable for vacation or year round living. The rear or southern elevation of the home is highlighted by an abundance of decks and glass. A minimum of windows are found on the north, east and west sides. The basement level has a large shop, storage and recreation areas, plus a bedroom. The first level living room is two steps up from the rest of the first floor, with two stories of glass on its southern wall. An angled wall lends charactor to the kitchen-dining area. The master suite occupies the entire second level with its own bath, dressing area, walk-in closet, storage nook and private deck.

First floor — 886 sq. ft.
Second floor — 456 sq. ft.
Basement — 886 sq. ft.

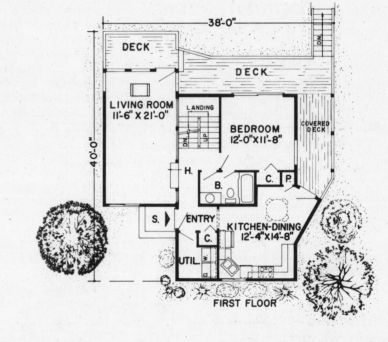

FIRST FLOOR

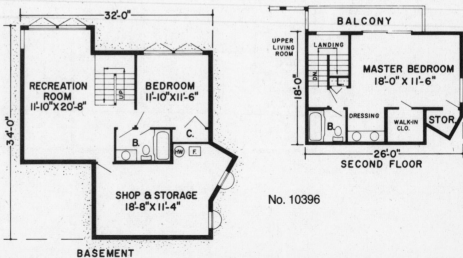

BASEMENT

SECOND FLOOR

No. 10396

Compact Charmer

No. 10789

From its traditional covered porch to its wide-open interior, this house is loaded with warmth and charm. A central foyer separates active and quiet areas. To the left, tucked behind the garage, three bedrooms and two full baths include the spacious master suite with its sunny bay sitting area and private patio access. You'll find another bay just off the family room, a perfect place to watch the birds as you wake up with your morning coffee. Clean-up chores won't be dull in the centrally-located kitchen with its corner sink surrounded by windows. And just steps away, the open living and dining rooms span the width of the house in a sunny, spacious arrangement that's ideal for entertaining.

Main living area — 1,692 sq. ft.
Garage — 540 sq. ft.

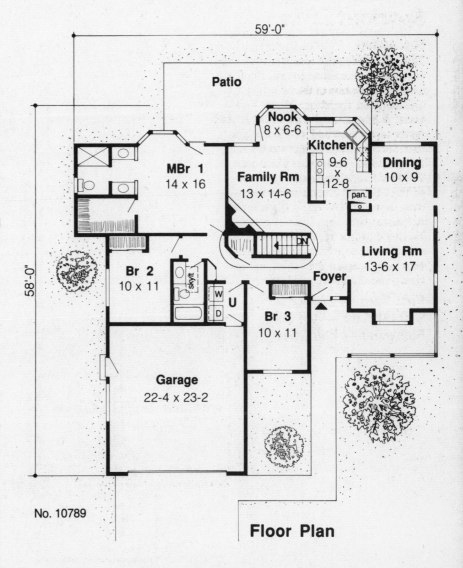

No. 10789

Floor Plan

Open Spaces

No. 91505

This spacious home achieves a wonderful, sun-washed atmosphere through intelligent space planning, generous windows, and vaulted ceilings. An angular, open staircase divides the two-story foyer from the vaulted living and dining rooms. A dramatic den just off the foyer features a window wall overlooking the street. And the informal area at the rear of the house is one huge expanse separated by a handy work island in the kitchen and high ceilings in the fireplaced family room. Enjoy the view from the balcony at the top of the stairs that links three bedrooms and two baths. In the master suite, vaulted ceilings, a skylit bath, and garden spa behind a glass block wall continue the wide-open atmosphere.

First floor — 1,152 sq. ft.
Second floor — 823 sq. ft.
Garage — 2-car

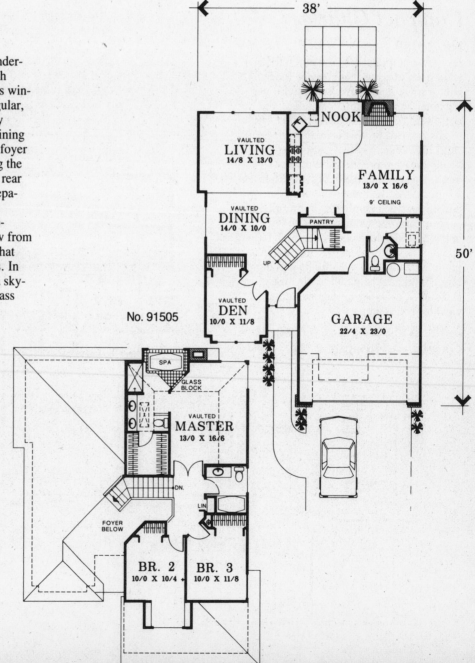

No. 91505

Planned for Privacy

No. 10797

The clapboard exterior of this one-level classic hints at the zoned plan you'll find inside. The quiet wing that houses three bedrooms, two full baths, and the handy laundry room juts out beyond the central entry, giving the facade a pleasing, interesting shape. The entry, the massive living room, and family room flow together. Sliding glass doors unite the family room with the backyard, adding to the spacious atmosphere. Even the kitchen shares the wide-open appeal, divided from the dining area by cabinets for easy meal service. There's loads of storage here, in the optional garage off the kitchen, the large closet and pantry in the family room, and the generous closets in each bedroom.

Main living area — 1,679 sq. ft.
Optional garage — 576 sq. ft.

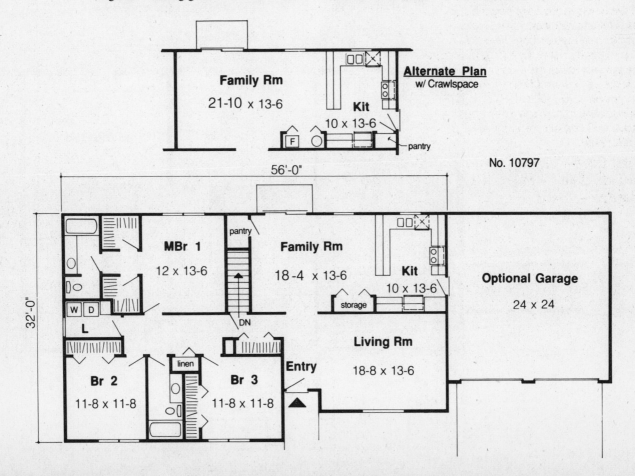

No Wasted Space

No. 90412

The open floor plan of this modified A-frame design virtually eliminated wasted hall space. The centrally located great room features a cathedral ceiling with exposed wood beams and large areas of fixed glass on both front and rear. Living and dining areas are virtually separated by a massive stone fireplace. The isolated master suite features a walk-in closet and sliding glass doors opening onto the front deck. A walk-thru utility room provides easy access from the carport and outside storage areas to the compact kitchen. On the opposite side of the great room are two additional bedrooms and a second full bath. A full-length deck and vertical wood siding with stone accents on the corners provide a rustic yet contemporary exterior. Specify crawlspace, basement or slab foundation when ordering.

Main living area — 1,454 sq. ft.

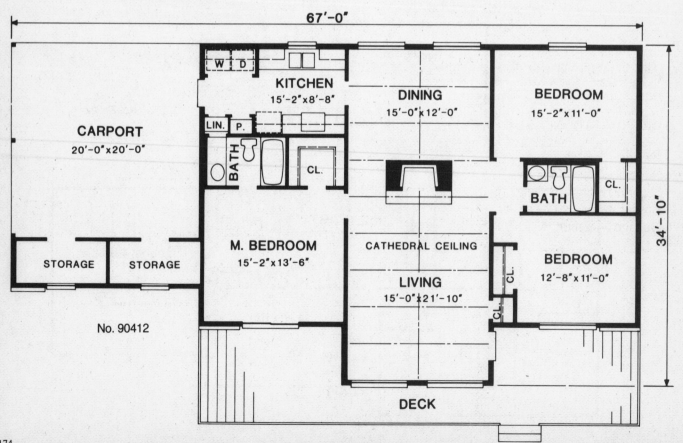

Formal Balance

No. 91502

This elegant home offers all the features demanded by today's busy family in a classic package. Look at the magnificent two-story foyer crowned by a towering palladium window, the special detailing under the eaves, and the traditional clapboard exterior adorned with a brick chimney. Inside, the foyer is flanked by the formal living room and the cozy family room with brick hearth. At mealtime, choose between the formal dining room that ajoins the living room, the sunny nook off the angular kitchen, or the patio just outside. Upstairs, three bedrooms include a magnificent master suite with garden spa and double vanities. And the bonus room provides plenty of room for growth.

First floor — 935 sq. ft.
Second floor — 772 sq. ft.
Bonus room — 177 sq. ft.
Garage — 2-car

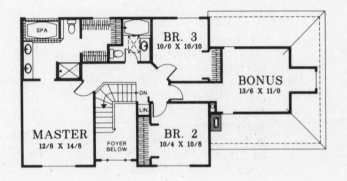

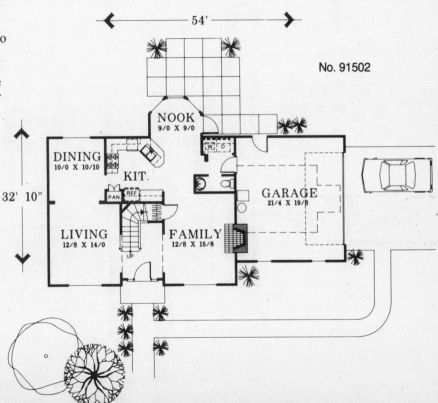

Living Areas Warmed by Massive Fireplace

No. 10752

Here's a handsome home for the family that enjoys one-level living. Skylights, sloping ceilings, and an absence of walls give active areas an irresistable, spacious atmosphere. And, with a floor-to-ceiling window wall in the living room and French doors in the dining room, interior spaces enjoy a pleasing unity with the great outdoors. Whether you're in the mood for formal or informal dining, the centrally located kitchen will make mealtime a breeze. Three bedrooms, each featuring a walk-in closet, occupy their own quiet wing off the foyer. The front bedrooms share a full bath with double vanities. The master suite at the rear of the house enjoys a private bath.

First floor — 1,705 sq. ft.
Garage — 488 sq. ft.

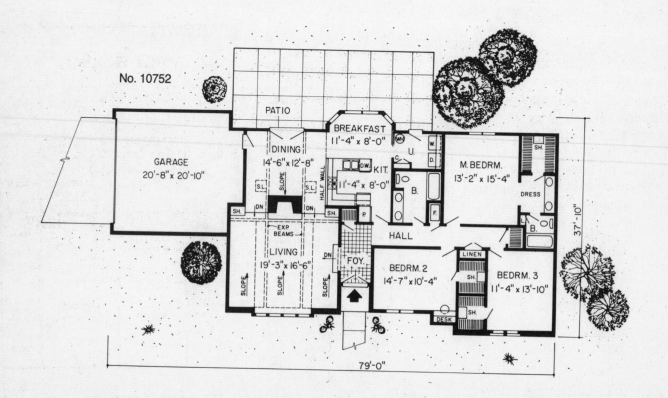

A Home for All Seasons

No. 90629

The natural cedar and stone exterior of this contemporary gem is virtually maintenance free, and its dramatic lines echo the excitement inside. There are so many luxurious touches in this plan: the two-story living room overlooked by an upper-level balcony, a massive stone wall that pierces the roof and holds two fireplaces, a kitchen oven and an outdoor barbecue. And, outdoor dining is a pleasure with the barbecue so handy to the kitchen. All the rooms boast outdoor decks, and each bedroom has its own. The front entrance, garage, a dressing room with bath, and laundry room occupy the lower level.

Main level — 1,001 sq. ft.
Upper level — 712 sq. ft.
Lower level — 463 sq. ft.

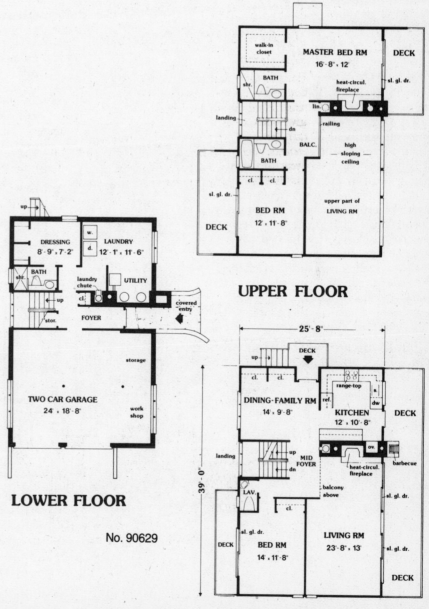

UPPER FLOOR

LOWER FLOOR

No. 90629

MAIN FLOOR

Built-In Beauty

No. 91507

From its skylit foyer to the garden spa in the master suite, this carefree home possesses a sunny charm you'll love coming home to. The living room features a bump-out window that enhances its wide-open arrangement with the formal dining room. At the rear of the house, the efficient island kitchen combines with a cheerful dining nook and fireplaced family room for a spacious, comfortable area just perfect for informal get-togethers. Down a short hall off the foyer, two bedrooms and a full bath flank the laundry room and handy garage entry. The master suite lies behind elegant double doors, boasting a luxurious, private bath with every amenity.

Main living area — 1,687 sq. ft.
Garage — 2-car

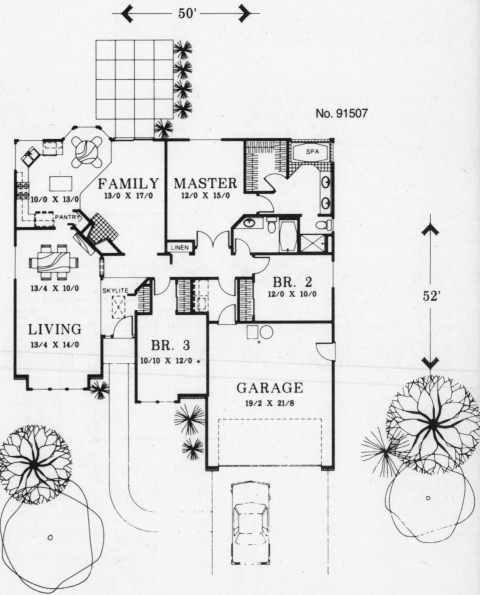

50'

No. 91507

FAMILY
13/0 X 17/0

MASTER
12/0 X 15/0

SPA

10/0 X 13/0

PANTRY

LINEN

13/4 X 10/0

BR. 2
12/0 X 10/0

SKYLITE

LIVING
13/4 X 14/0

BR. 3
10/10 X 12/0

GARAGE
19/2 X 21/8

52'

Unlimited Options

No. 10793

Here's a home designed to adapt to your needs — and your budget. A handsome, traditional exterior faced with clapboard siding is an attractive introduction to this comfortable home. Step through the front door to a spacious living room that flows into the rear-facing dining room for a wide-open feeling accentuated by sliding glass doors. You'll love the efficient galley kitchen, with its built-in pantry and handy backyard access. A full bath serves the three bedrooms, which are tucked down a short hall for a private atmosphere. An attached garage and full basement give you lots of room for storage and workshop space. But if you want to save on costs, eliminate the garage, and choose the alternate crawlspace plan.

Main living area — 1,248 sq. ft.
Optional garage — 484 sq. ft.

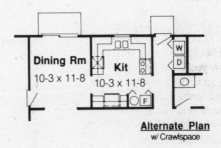

Alternate Plan
w/ Crawlspace

No. 10793

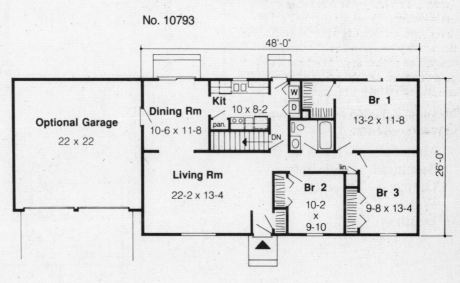

Have Your Morning Coffee on the Sundeck

No. 90911

If you've been searching for a contemporary home at a price you can afford, you must consider this exciting model. Interesting exterior angles are enhanced by the clean lines of cedar plank siding. The front entrance is sheltered by a roof extension and leads in to a sunny foyer. Walk up to the main level, brightened by lots of oversized windows. The big double garage includes a large storage and workshop area with convenient access to the rear yard. If you like modern styling, this three-bedroom beauty will reflect your good taste.

Main floor — 1,205 sq. ft.
Basement — 550 sq. ft.
Garage — 728 sq.ft.
Width — 46 ft.
Depth — 32 ft.

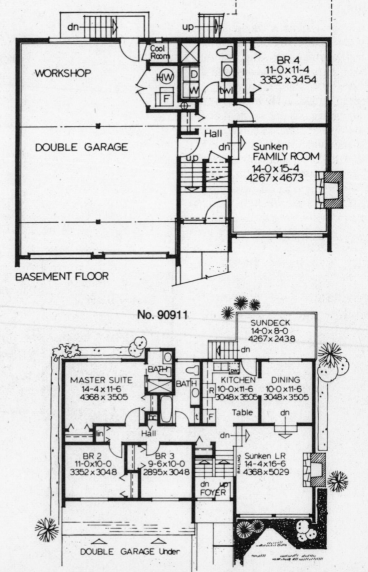

Compact Home for a Small Space

No. 90500

A massive bay window is the dominant feature in the facade of this cozy home with attached two-car garage. From the entry, there are three ways to walk. Turn left into the fireplaced living room and adjoining dining room. Or walk straight into the kitchen and breakfast nook, which extends to a covered porch. Step down the hall on the right to the master suite, full bath, and a second bedroom. The TV room, which can double as a third bedroom, completes the circular floor plan in this convenient, one-level abode.

Floor area — 1,299 sq. ft.

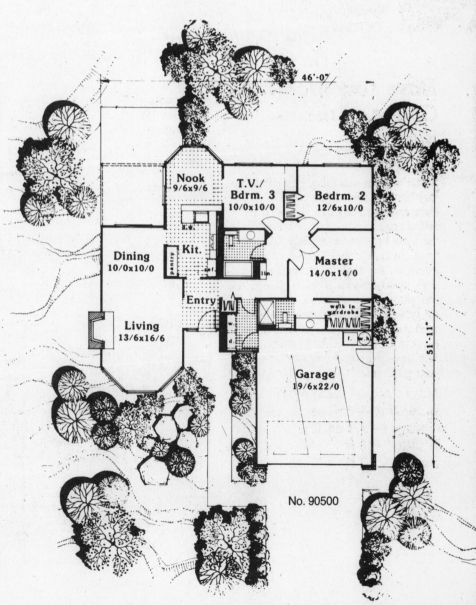

Nook
9/6x9/6

T.V./
Bdrm. 3
10/0x10/0

Bedrm. 2
12/6x10/0

Dining
10/0x10/0

Kit.

Master
14/0x14/0

Entry

walk in wardrobe

Living
13/6x16/6

Garage
19/6x22/0

46'-07"

51'-11"

No. 90500

Mud Room Separates Garage and Kitchen

No. 9812

Gardening and woodworking tools will find a home in the storage closet of the useful mud room in this rustic detailed ranch. Besides incorporating a laundry area, the mud room will prove invaluable as a place for removing snowy boots and draining wet umbrellas. The family room appendages the open kitchen and flows outward to the stone terrace. The master bedroom is furnished with a private bath and protruding closet space, and the living room retains a formality by being situated to the left of the entryway.

First floor — 1,396 sq. ft.
Basement — 1,396 sq. ft.
Garage — 484 sq. ft.

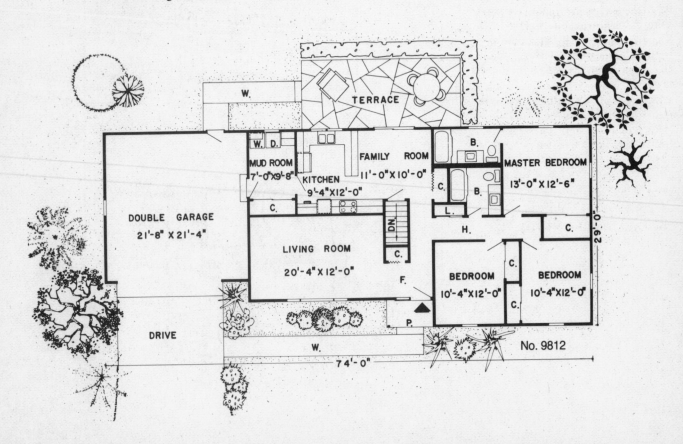

Design Portrays
Expensive Look

No. 90040

Inside the front entrance and beyond the foyer, a square reception hall divides traffic to either living or service area. Located here is a powder room for easy guest use. To the left the 20 x 13 living room with its 8-foot wide bank of front windows, log burning fireplace and French doors to the connecting porch provides adequate, comfortable space for three-bedroom living. Their use will continue to be appreciated over the years of the day-to-day living. The curving staircase to the second floor leads to the sleeping level. To the right is a large storage area. A space to the rear could, by day, be finished as a den or office which still would leave plenty of storage. Two baths offer more than adequate service for the three bedrooms. A round master bath is located in the turret.

First floor — 1,069 sq. ft.
Second floor — 948 sq. ft.

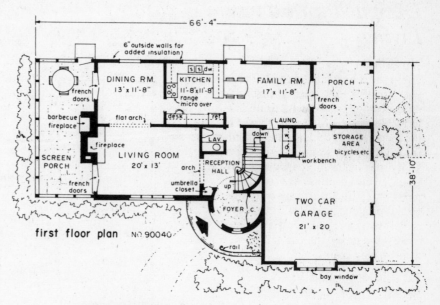

first floor plan   NO 90040

No. 90040

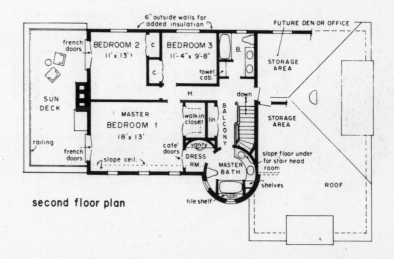

second floor plan

Designed for Family Living

No. 90604

The grand, circular staircase will charm your guests as they enter this traditional three-bedroom loaded with family features. Flanked by formal dining and living rooms, the foyer leads straight into the family living area of the house, with utility room entry for muddy kids and grocery-laden parents. The cozy family room with raised hearth is a comfortable center for group activities. Four bedrooms, two baths, and closets galore make this a house you can enjoy for many, happy years.

**First floor — 952 sq. ft.
Second floor — 892 sq. ft.
(excluding garage, laundry, storage)**

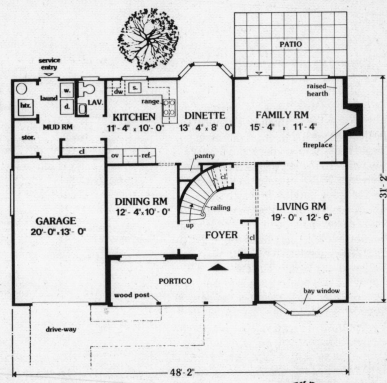

No. 90604

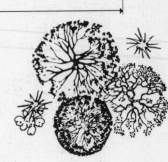

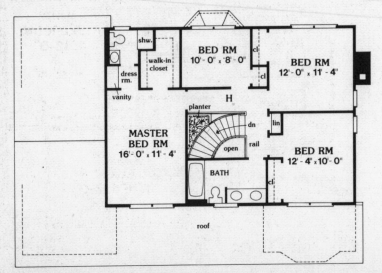

SECOND FLOOR

Glass Walls Seem to Enlarge Front Living Areas

No. 10482

The second floor of this original design contains two bedrooms plus a shared walk-through path. Fronting the second floor are the stairway and a balcony which overlooks the glass-walled living room. The dining room also boasts a front glass wall and opens onto the efficient U-shaped kitchen. The full bath on the first floor may be accessed privately through the master bedroom or off the central hall. The laundry room, which also includes the utility area, is conveniently located between the kitchen and the master bedroom.

First floor — 966 sq.ft.
Second floor — 455 sq.ft.
Garage — 353 sq.ft.

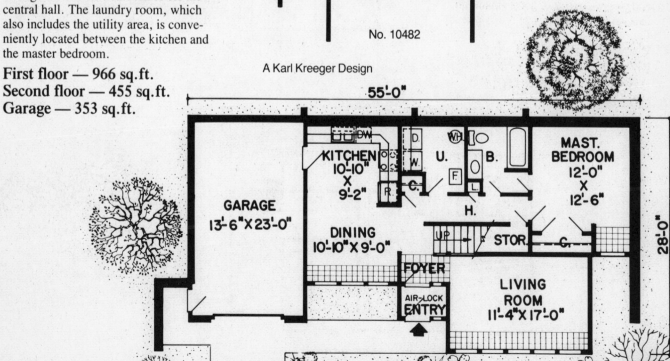

BEDROOM 3
9'-10"
X
11'-10"

B.

BEDROOM 2
9'-10"
X
11'-10"

ST.

H.

C.

DN.

C.

OPEN TO LIVING
ROOM BELOW

SECOND
FLOOR

No. 10482

A Karl Kreeger Design

55'-0"

GARAGE
13'-6" X 23'-0"

KITCHEN
10'-10"
X
9'-2"

D.

W.

U.

WH

B.

MAST.
BEDROOM
12'-0"
X
12'-6"

C.

F.

DINING
10'-10" X 9'-0"

H.

UP

STOR.

C.

FOYER

AIR-LOCK
ENTRY

LIVING
ROOM
11'-4" X 17'-0"

28'-0"

FIRST FLOOR

Unique Floor Plan Accommodates Larger Family

No. 10546

This four-bedroom beauty offers all you could want in a larger house and more. Three of the bedrooms and the dining areas are located on the upper floor, with the primary living areas on the lower floor. The family room has a fireplace and sloped ceiling. A bedroom and full bath on the lower floor provides privacy for guests.

Upper floor — 1,504 sq. ft.
Lower floor — 268 sq. ft.
Basement — 396 sq. ft.
Garage — 440 sq. ft.

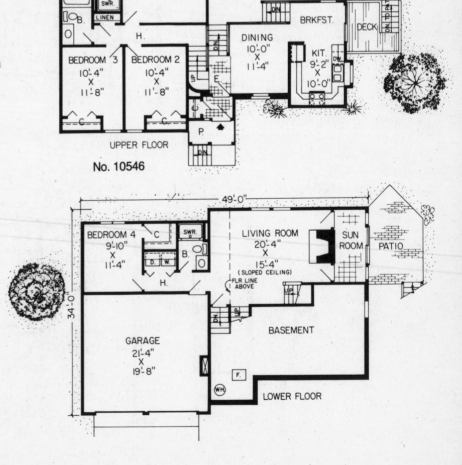

No. 10546

UPPER FLOOR

M. BEDROOM 14'-4" X 13'-4"
LIVING ROOM BELOW
BRKFST.
DECK
DINING 10'-0" X 11'-4"
KIT. 9'-2" X 10'-0"
BEDROOM 3 10'-4" X 11'-8"
BEDROOM 2 10'-4" X 11'-8"

BEDROOM 4 9'-10" X 11'-4"
LIVING ROOM 20'-4" X 15'-4" (SLOPED CEILING)
SUN ROOM
PATIO
GARAGE 21'-4" X 19'-8"
BASEMENT
LOWER FLOOR
49'-0"
34'-0"

Bays Add Beauty and Living Space

No. 90607

The welcoming warmth that most Traditional houses seem to exude is especially evident in this center hall, four-bedroom residence. Just off the two-story foyer, the formal living room features a heat-circulating fireplace. Ionic columns and a semi-circular window wall give the dining room a classic grace. The U-shaped kitchen opens to the fireplaced family room. Off the foyer, there are two bedrooms and two baths. Two bedrooms upstairs share a bath.

First floor — 1,515 sq. ft.
Second floor — 530 sq. ft.

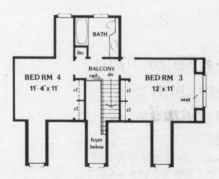

SECOND FLOOR PLAN

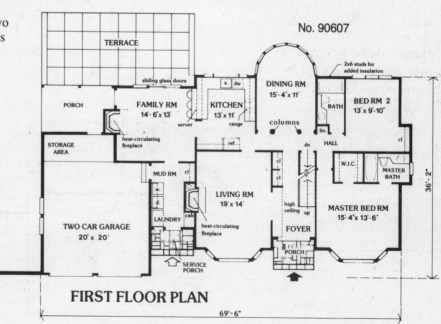

No. 90607

FIRST FLOOR PLAN

Order Your Blueprints Now!

Order number # 375186

You'll Get Results Fast-- And Save Money, Too!! -- With Our Complete, Accurate Professional Blueprints. I Know You'll Love Tour New Home. Sincerely, Whitney Garlinghouse

How Many Sets of Plans Will You Need?

Experience shows that the **Standard 8-Set Construction Package** is best. You'll speed every step of construction and avoid costly building errors by ordering enough sets to go around. And, usually everyone wants their own set. Consider your lending institution, general contractor and all of his subcontractors; foundation; framing; electrical; plumbing; heating/air conditioning; drywall; and finish carpenters—as well as a set for you.

Minimum 5-Set Construction Package gives an efficient planner a choice. Although eight sets relieves you of worry about sets being lost or ruined on the job, you can carefully hand sets down as work progresses and might have enough copies to go around with the five set package.

One Complete Set of Blueprints lets you study the blueprints, so you can plan your dream home. But, keep in mind . . . One set is never enough for actually building your home.

✳ Here's What You Get!

Our accurate and complete blueprints contain everything you need to begin building your dream home:

- Front, rear, and both side views of the house (elevations)
- Floor plans for all levels
- Roof plan
- Foundation plan
- Universal Plot plan
- Typical wall sections (sectional slices throughout the home)
- Kitchen and bathroom cabinet details
- Fireplace details (where applicable)
- Stair details (where applicable)
- Locations of electrical fixtures and components
- Specifications and contract form
- Energy Conservation Specifications Guide

Please note: All plans are drawn to conform with one or more of the industry's major national building standards. However, local building codes may differ from national standards. We recommend that you check with your local building officials.   B20

Remember to Order a Materials List!

Our materials list for your home plan will help you save money! This helpful list is available at a small additional charge and gives the quantity, dimensions and specifications for all major materials needed to build your home (small hardware like nails, screws, etc. are omitted). With this valuable list, you'll get faster and more accurate bids from your contractors and building suppliers. In addition, you'll avoid paying for unnecessary materials and waste.

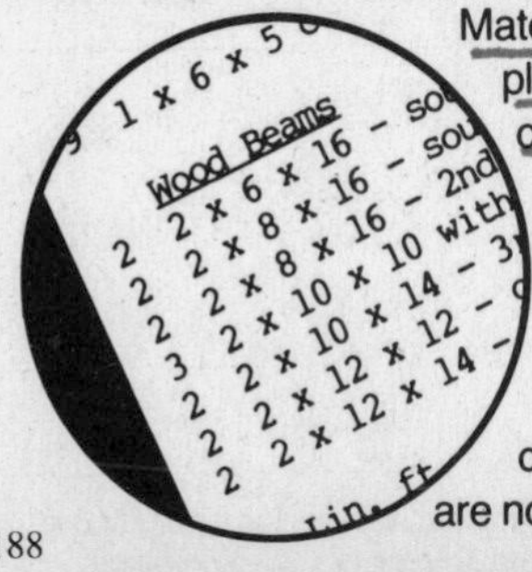

Materials lists are available for all home plans except where otherwise indicated, but can only be ordered along with a set of home plans. **Please Note:** Due to differences in local building codes, regional requirements and builder preferences . . . electrical, plumbing, and heating/air conditioning equipment requirements are not provided as part of the material list.

1 x 6 x 5
Wood Beams
2 x 4 x 16 - so
2 x 8 x 16 - sou
2 x 8 x 16 - 2nd
2 x 10 x 10 with
2 x 10 x 14 - 3
2 x 12 x 12 -
3 2 x 12 x 14 -
2 2 x 12 x 14 -
in. ft.

Discover Reverse Plans at no extra charge!

You may find that a particular house would suit your taste or fit your lot better if it were "reversed." A reverse plan turns the design end-for-end. That is, if the garage is shown on the left side and the bedrooms on the right, the reverse plan will place the garage on the right side and the bedrooms on the left. To see quickly how a design will look in reverse, hold your book up to a mirror.

If you want to build your Garlinghouse Home in reverse, then order your plans reversed. You'll receive one mirror-image, reversed set of plans (with "backwards" lettering and dimensions) as a master guide for you and your builder. The remaining sets in your order are then sent as shown in our publication for ease in reading the lettering and dimensions. These "as shown" sets will all be marked "REVERSED" with a special stamp to eliminate confusion on the job site. **Reverse plans are available only on multiple set orders.**

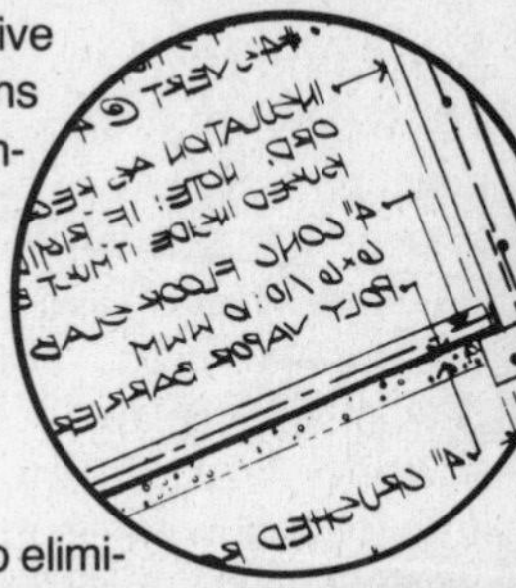

Modify Your Garlinghouse Home Plan!

Your custom dream home can be as wonderful as you want. Easy modifications, such as minor non-structural changes and simple building material substitutions, can be made by any competent builder without the need for blueprint revisions.

However, if you are considering making major changes to your design, we strongly recommend that you seek the services of an architect or professional designer. Even these expensive professional services will cost less with our complete, detailed blueprints as a starting point.

Reproducible Mylars Make Plan Modifications Easier!

Ask about our Reproducible Mylars for your home design. They're inexpensive and provide a design professional with a way to make custom changes directly to our home plans and then print as many copies as you need of the modified design. It's a perfect way to create a truly custom home! Prices range from $340 to $415 plus mailing charges. **Call 1-800-235-5700 to find out more about our Reproducible Mylars.** Please Note: Reproducible mylars are not available for plans numbered 90,000 and above, or for plans numbered 19,000 through 19,999.

PRICE SCHEDULE

One Complete Set of Blueprints	$125.00
Minimum Construction Package (5 Sets)	$170.00
Standard Construction Package (8 Sets)	$200.00
Each Additional Set Ordered With One of the Above Packages	$20.00
Materials List (with plan order only)	$15.00

215

Prices are subject to change without notice

Important Shipping Information

Your order receives our immediate attention! However, please allow 10 working days from our receipt of your order for normal UPS delivery. You can call in your credit card order TOLL FREE and avoid the additional mail delay for your order to reach us.

Note that UPS will deliver **only** to street addresses and rural route delivery boxes and **not** to Post Office Box Numbers. Please print your complete street address. If no one is home during the day, you may use your work address to insure prompt delivery.

We **MUST** ship First Class Mail to Alaska or Hawaii, APO, FPO, or a Post Office Box. Please note the higher cost for First Class Mail.

Domestic Shipping

UPS Ground Service	$5.75 *+1.00*
First Class Mail	$7.75
Express Delivery Service	Call for details 1-800-235-5700

overnight $25

International Orders & Shipping

If you are ordering from outside the United States, please note that your check, money order, or international money transfer **must be payable in U.S. currency.**

We ship all international orders via Air Parcel Post for delivery (surface mail is extremely slow). Please refer to the schedule below for the mailing charge on your order and substitute this amount for the usual mailing charges for domestic orders.

International Shipping

	One Set	Multiple Sets
Canada	$5.75	$9.75
Mexico & Caribbean Nations	$16.50	$39.50
All other Nations	$18.50	$50.00

Canadian orders are now duty free.

For Fastest Service...
ORDER TOLL FREE
1-800-235-5700

Connecticut, Alaska, Hawaii, & all foreign residents call 1-203-632-0500. Please have your credit card and order code number ready when you call.

FAX: 1-203-632-0712

BLUEPRINT ORDER FORM

GARLINGHOUSE

Send your Check, Money Order or Credit Card information to:
The Garlinghouse Company
34 Industrial Park Place, P.O. Box 1717
Middletown, CT 06457

Order Code No.

H90S4

PLAN NO._____

QTY.   ☐ as shown   ☐ reversed

_____ 1 Set Pkg. **($125.00)** . . . . . . = $_____

_____ 5 Set Pkg. **($170.00)** . . . . . . = $_____

_____ 8 Set Pkg. **($200.00)** . . . . . . = $_____

_____ Additional Sets **($20.00 ea.)** . = $_____

_____ Materials List **($15.00)** . . . . . = $_____

Shipping Charges (see charts) . . . . . = $_____

Subtotal . . . . = $_____

Sales Tax* . . . . = $_____
*Kansas residents add 5.25% sales tax
Connecticut residents add 8% sales tax

TOTAL AMOUNT ENCLOSED $ [_____]

Thank You for Your Order!

BILL TO:

Name_____
                    Please Print
Address_____

City & State_____ Zip_____

Phone (_____)_____

SHIP TO:

Name_____
                    Please Print
Address_____

City & State_____ Zip_____

Phone (_____)_____

METHOD OF PAYMENT: ☐ Check   ☐ Money Order

Charge to: ☐ Visa   ☐ MasterCard

Signature_____ Exp. Date____/____

Builder's Library

The books on this page were written with the professional home builder in mind. They are all comprehensive information sources for contractors or for those beginners who wish to build like contractors.

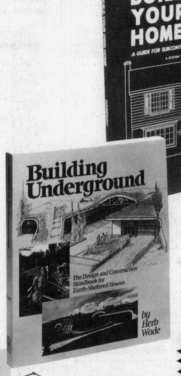

◄ 2518 Build Your Own Home An authoritative guide on how to be your own general contractor. This book goes through the step-by-step process of building a house with special emphasis on the business aspects such as financing, scheduling, permits, insurance, and more. Furthermore, it gives you an understanding of what to expect out of your various subcontractors so that you can properly orchestrate their work. 112 pp.; Holland House (paperback) **$12.95**

► 2600. Building Underground This has been compiled on earth sheltered homes, built all over North America—homes that are spacious, attractive and comfortable in every way. These homes are more energy efficient than above ground houses. Physical security, low operating costs, and noise reduction further enhance their attractiveness. 304 pp.; 85 photos; 112 illus.; Rodale Press (paperback) **$14.95**

from the Leading Publishers in the Do-It-Yourself Industry!!!

◄ 2596 How To Get It Built No matter how small or how large your construction project is, building will be easier with this informative guidebook. This text was prepared for people involved in building on a non-professional basis. Guidelines have been carefully prepared to follow step-by-step construction-cost savings methods. Written by an architect/contractor, this book offers home construction owners the planning, construction and cost saving solutions to his own building needs. 238 pp.; over 300 illus.; (paperback) Hashagen **$18.00**

► 2508. Modern Plumbing All aspects of plumbing installation, service, and repair are presented here in illustrated, easy-to-follow text. This book contains all the information needed for vocational competence, including the most up-to-date tools, materials, and practices. 300 pp.; over 700 illus.; Goodheart-Willcox (hardcover) **$19.96**

▲ 2607. Radon: The Invisible Threat This book will help you become more aware of this potentially harmful situation, with easy, step-by-step instructions, to help you detect the presence of Radon Gas in your home. Also included is a simple test that could prevent your home from becoming a victim of this environmental hazard. 224 pp.; Rodale (paperback) **$12.95**

▲ **2546. Blueprint Reading for Construction** This combination text and workbook shows and tells how to read residential, commercial, and light industrial prints. With an abundance of actual drawings from industry, you learn step by step about each component of a set of blueprints, including even cost estimating. 336 pp.; Goodheart-Willcox (spiral bound) **$21.28**

▲ **2570. Modern Masonry** Everything you will ever need to know about concrete, masonry, and brick, is included in this book. Forms construction, concrete reinforcement, proper foundation construction, and bricklaying are among the topics covered in step-by-step detail. An excellent all-round reference and guide. 256 pp.; 700 illus.; Goodheart-Willcox (hardcover) **$19.96**

▼ **2514. The Underground House Book** For anyone seriously interested in building and living in an underground home, this book tells it all. Aesthetic considerations, building codes, site planning, financing, insurance, planning and decorating considerations, maintenance costs, soil, excavation, landscaping, water considerations, humidity control, and specific case histories are among the many facets of underground living dealt with in this publication. 208 pp.; 140 illus.; Garden Way (paperback) **$10.95**

▼ **2504. Architecture, Residential Drawing and Design** An excellent text that explains all the fundamentals on how to create a complete set of construction drawings. Specific areas covered include proper design and planning considerations, foundation plans, floor plans, elevations, stairway details, electrical plans, plumbing plans, etc. 492 pp.; over 800 illus.; Goodheart-Willcox (hardcover) **$26.60**

▲ **2510. Modern Carpentry** A complete guide to the "nuts and bolts" of building a home. This book explains all about building materials, framing, trim work, insulation, foundations, and much more. A valuable text and reference guide. 492 pp.; over 1400 illus.; Goodheart-Willcox (hardcover) **$25.20**

▲ **2506. House Wiring Simplified** This book teaches all the fundamentals of modern house wiring; shows how it's done with easy-to-understand drawings. A thorough guide to the materials and practices for safe, efficient installation of home electrical systems. 176 pp.; 384 illus.; Goodheart-Willcox (hardcover) **$10.00**

▼ **2544. Solar Houses** An examination of solar homes from the standpoint of lifestyle. This publication shows you through photographs, interviews, and practical information, what a solar lifestyle involves, how owners react to it, and what the bottom-line economics are. Included are 130 floor plans and diagrams which give you a clear idea of how various "active" and "passive" solar systems work. 160 pp.; 370 illus. Pantheon (paperback) **$9.95**

▼ **2592. How to Design & Build Decks & Patios** Learn how to create decks and patios to suit every type of lot and lifestyle. This fully illustrated source book includes detailed information on design and construction as well as special charts on building and paving materials. Full color, 112 pp.; Ortho (paperback) **$7.95**

2586. How to Design & Remodel Kitchens — This book takes you through steps beginning with evaluating your present kitchen and designing a new one to hiring a contractor or doing the work yourself. It offers solid information on the things you need to know to create the kitchen that best fits your needs. Full color charts and illustrations. 96 pp.; Successful (paperback) **$6.95**

▲ **2612. Baths** With charts and illustrations provided, BATHS gives tips on new storage ideas, suggestions on whirlpools and saunas, and a tour of 30 of the best-designed baths in the United States. Assistance is provided in the form of addresses of leading manufacturers and helpful organizations, to aid you in the remodeling of your bath. 154 pp.; Rodale (paperback) **$12.95**

▼ **2611. Tile It Up! Plumb It Up!** Using the many illustrations and the easy steps included in this valuable book, you will be able to work just like the professionals. This book provides step-by-step instructions on plumbing and tiling, enabling the do-it-yourselfer to complete these projects with a minimum of time providing maximum results. 43 pp.; XS Books (paperback) **$6.95**

▼ **2516. Building Consultant** The new home buyer's bible to home construction. This encyclopedia of home building explains in comprehensive detail about all the various elements that go into a completed house. It enables you to deal with the construction of your new home in a meaningful way that will avoid costly errors, whether you use a contractor or build it yourself. 188 pp.; Holland House (paperback) **$12.95**

Builder's Library order form

Yes! send me the following books:

book order no.	price
_____	$ _____
_____	$ _____
_____	$ _____
_____	$ _____
_____	$ _____
_____	$ _____

Postage & handling (one book only)	$ _____1.75
Add 50¢ postage & handling for each additional book	$ _____
Canada add $1.50 per book	
Resident sales tax: Kansas (5.25%)	$ _____
Connecticut (8%)	$ _____
TOTAL ENCLOSED	

No C.O.D. orders accepted; U.S. funds only.
prices subject to change without notice

My Shipping Address is:
(please print)

Name _____

Address _____

City _____

State _____ Zip _____

Send your order to:
(With check or money order enclosed)

**The Garlinghouse Company
34 Industrial Park Place
P.O. Box 1717
Middletown, Connecticut 06457**

For Faster Service . . .
CHARGE IT!   (203) 632-0500

☐ MasterCard   ☐ Visa

Exp.
Date _____

Card # _____

Signature _____

▼ **2604. The Low Maintenance House**
At last, an idea-packed book that will save you thousands of hours on home maintenance. It's an essential planning guide for anyone building a home. Discover new as well as time-tested techniques and products for cutting down the time, and slashing the money you spend to clean and repair your home . . . from roof to basement, from front yard to backyard garden. This book will earn its price, and your thanks, over and over again. 314 pp.; Rodale (hardback) **$19.95**

▲ **2605. Contracting Your Home** With over 150 illustrations, this guide offers many suggestions and ideas on contracting your own home. Many forms you can copy and re-use are provided, giving checklists and a glossary of terms used by the professionals, as well as all the necessary estimating forms. 279 pp.; Betterway Publications (paperback) **$18.95**

▼ **2608. Cut Your Electric Bill in Half**
With assistance from this book, you may be able to cut your future electric bills by up to 80%! With tables outlining the effective use of all your home appliances and recommendations for money-saving appliances, this book is a MUST for the budget-conscious household. 160 pp.; Rodale (paperback) **$9.95**

▲ **2542. Designing and Building a Solar House** Written by one of America's foremost authorities on solar architecture. It is a practical "how-to" guide that clearly demonstrates the most sensible ways to marry good house design with contemporary solar technology. Included is a thorough discussion of both "active" and "passive" solar systems, and even a listing of today's leading solar homes. 288 pp.; 400 illus.; Garden Way (paperback) **$15.95**

▼ **2610. The Backyard Builder** Here is a step-by-step guide for over 150 projects for the gardener and homeowner, accompanied by over 100 photos, 400 illustrations, materials lists and shopping guides. You are sure to find many useful, attractive projects that the entire family can help with. 656 pp.; Rodale (hardcover) **$21.95**

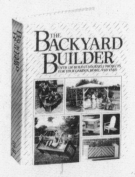

▲ **2606. Building Fences** With emphasis on function and style, this guide to a wide variety of fence-building is a solid how-to book. With easy-to-read instructions, and plenty of illustrations, this book is a must for the professional and the do-it-yourselfer. 188 pp.; Williamson Publishing (paperback) **$13.95**